THE 1% WELLNESS
EXPERIMENT

WELBECK
BALANCE

Published in 2023 by Welbeck Balance
An imprint of Welbeck Non-Fiction Limited
Part of Welbeck Publishing Group
Offices in: London – 20 Mortimer Street, London W1T 3JW &
Sydney – Level 17, 207 Kent St, Sydney NSW 2000 Australia
www.welbeckpublishing.com

A CIP catalogue record for this book is available from the British Library.

ISBN
978-1-80129-294-8

Typeset by Lapiz Digital Services
Printed in Great Britain by CPI Group (UK) Ltd

10 9 8 7 6 5 4 3 2 1

MIX
Paper | Supporting
responsible forestry
FSC® C171272

THE 1% WELLNESS EXPERIMENT

Micro-gains to Change Your Life in 10 Minutes a Day

Gabrielle Treanor

WELBECK
BALANCE

To you, for being willing, for wanting,
for knowing you deserve to just try.

CONTENTS

INTRODUCTION

WHAT IS THE 1%
WELLNESS EXPERIMENT?

Welcome to *The 1% Wellness Experiment*!

As the title describes, this book's premise is centred on entering into an experiment to boost your wellness that takes up just 1% of your waking day. Based on a 16-hour day (which allows for the recommended 8 hours of sleep), 1% is 9.6 minutes, which I've rounded up to ten minutes for ease.

There are enough experiments included for you to do one for every day of the month. These experiments vary from addressing how you relate to the people around you, how you start and end your day, and how you treat yourself, to designing your environment, exploring your mindset, and learning how to feel calm, in control and joyful. We explore techniques, strategies and tools drawn from popular therapeutic practices, such as cognitive behavioural therapy, solution-focused therapy, acceptance and commitment therapy, and compassion-focused therapy as well as positive psychology.

The experiments explore areas that affect your day-to-day life and wellbeing and cover topics such as boundaries, comparison, self-care, mindset, sleep, habits, self-talk and many more. Each experiment is designed to get you thinking and taking action, so that you *can* change your life in just ten minutes a day.

I've called these ideas, tasks or exercises "experiments" for a very important reason: because you really are *trying them out*.

The idea is to see how you get on with each one without pressure for it to be the perfect solution to all your wellness troubles. Because, to be blunt, there is no perfect solution to all your wellness troubles – and please be wary of anyone who says they can make anything in life perfect!

I've put into practice every single one of these experiments, many times. Some are firm favourites, which I've now woven into the fabric of my day; others I make use of as and when I want or need. I've benefited from all of them, which is why I'm sharing them with you. I don't expect you to love them all, but through your own exploration of each experiment I hope you will find what really connects with you.

By the end of your experimenting, you will be equipped with a bespoke toolkit that will enable you to:

- gain clarity on what you want and need (and better communicate that with others)
- tap into your inner wisdom, strength and confidence
- be kinder to yourself and take better care of your mental and emotional health
- be more present, calmer and happier.

You can either dip into or make regular use of these practices as best suits your needs. With the guidance of *The 1% Wellness Experiment* you get to find what works for *you* – the unique, quirky, flawed, glorious human that is you.

Little things make a big difference

Just ten minutes, just 1% of your day. How can such a teeny amount of time possibly make a difference? Let's consider the idea of "marginal gains" for a moment…

In 2003, Performance Director Dave Brailsford was given the task of improving British Cycling's performance when their record was woeful.[1] Since 1920, they had won just one Olympic gold medal (Chris Boardman in 1992[2]), and in 110 years no British cyclist had won the Tour de France.[3]

Brailsford applied a strategy of marginal gains – he looked at every aspect of British Cycling with the aim of improving each aspect by 1%.[4] He believed that the accumulation of all those 1% tweaks would make a significant difference.

There were the technical adjustments you'd expect, such as making bikes, clothing and equipment as aerodynamic as possible. And there were the seemingly very small changes, such as washing hands more thoroughly to minimize the spread of germs, and finding the most suitable pillow and mattress for a good night's sleep (and taking those specific items on the road to competitions).[5]

These and many more tweaks added up to have a big impact. Five years after Brailsford became Performance Director, British Cycling won more than half of the road and track cycling gold medals up for grabs at the 2008 Beijing Olympics.[6] In 2012, Bradley Wiggins became the first Brit to win the Tour de France,[7] and at the London Olympics of the same year the British team matched their Beijing gold medal haul, while the

British Paralympic team won a whopping 17 road and track gold medals.[1]

The 1% had well and truly added up. Dave Brailsford and his team hadn't gone for monumental, revolutionary changes, instead they tweaked; and bit by bit those small adjustments built up to make a significant difference.

And that's what we're going to do – with ten minutes or 1% of your day. To quote Dave Brailsford, we're going to, "Forget about perfection; focus on progression and compound the improvements."[5]

HOW THIS BOOK WILL CHANGE YOUR LIFE

It's a grand claim, isn't it? So, let's be clear. I'm not saying this book will make your life super-shiny, perfect, and easy-breezy – because, sadly, no book can do that. Nothing and no one can make that promise, because nobody's life *is* super-shiny, perfect, and easy-breezy; that's simply not the human experience.

And, it's not solely on you as an individual to change your life. There are societal structures that are responsible for the difficulties many of us experience in life, particularly members of marginalized communities; and challenging these systems is crucial to making the world we live in a fairer, more equitable place.

However, while we work to change how our society is set up, there are also small and powerful actions we can take to make a positive difference to our own lives on a daily basis.

But, *can* this book change your life? I think it just might.

WHY I WROTE THIS BOOK

While I might describe myself now as a "recovering perfectionist", for much of my life I was very much in the grip of perfectionism. For me, perfectionism is less about wanting to do things perfectly and more about *really* not wanting to get things wrong. Or to make a mistake. Or to be rubbish at something (even though it's very likely you're going to be rubbish, at first, when trying something new). Or to mess up in front of other people. Or to just not be very good in front of other people. And when I did fail to do things well the first time, or (thought I) looked foolish or struggled with something new (which was inevitable because I'm human), I went all in on the self-criticism (known as "self-oriented perfectionism"[1]).

We take on perfectionism as a safety mechanism. If we only do what we're pretty sure we're going to succeed at (or at least not be useless at), we can avoid the (perhaps perceived) discomfort of failure, criticism, judgement, being laughed at and, depending on the circumstances, avoid a real threat to our personal safety. As children, we learn from family, school, friends, the media how emotionally unsafe it feels to get things wrong; we believe we must meet their expectations (this is known as "socially prescribed perfectionism"[8])... even if we aren't in any kind of physical danger.

When we have perfectionist tendencies, it makes us wary of trying new things as we can't be sure of how well it's going to go. If we don't think we'll like something or that we might struggle with it and fail, we won't try it. Procrastination is often grounded in perfectionism.

If we do take the plunge and have a go, we put so much pressure on ourselves to do well it sucks all the joy out of any new experience. And if we don't "succeed" (whatever that may look like), we take it as proof of our personal failing and a reminder of why we shouldn't try in the first place.

This fear of being rubbish at something new, of failing or getting it wrong, got in my way for a long time – until I took a different approach.

A new approach

What if I treated the new experience as an experiment rather than as a challenge? What if I told myself that, *I'm going to try doing a thing (whatever it might be) without any specific expectations of the outcome? This way, there is no success or failure – there's no hitting a target or achieving a goal – so I can't get it wrong.*

Coming at a new experience from this perspective takes the pressure right off. It allows me to try and learn without the belief I have to get it right from the start. I can't be scared of messing up because it's all just an experiment!

Taking this approach was like turning a key in a lock. It gave me permission to try things I didn't know I could do because it was no longer about succeeding or failing, it was about exploring a possibility – trying something out and seeing how I got on. I could pull on my experience, see where I needed help, what I needed to tweak, and then decide if I wanted to work on improving or cast this experiment aside and move on.

This book is packed full of "experiments" – a way to test or try out ideas that have the power to make a real difference if you fully embrace and integrate them into your life. You don't even need to implement every experiment to see changes in your life. You might find that just one on its own has a massive impact, if it hits the right mark for you.

The little perfectionist voice in my head still likes to pipe up with the old fearful thoughts of looking stupid, and getting things wrong but now I can reassure her that we're just experimenting. Having shared this experimental approach with my coaching clients over the years, I've seen how powerful it is in allowing people to stop procrastinating, move past their fears and do what it is they want to do and what could benefit them if they just allow themselves to try.

It's all an experiment

With these experiments, you will be spending just ten minutes of your waking day on a small, yet powerful, step toward improving your wellbeing and your life. Will ten minutes alone turn your world upside down? No (but are you even looking to turn your world upside down?), but taking this action will have a positive impact on your day-to-day living.

The experiments aren't designed to be one-offs. The ones that you find enjoyable, useful, beneficial and make a difference, you'll practise again. And again. As you keep practising, the ten minutes will add up and, as they do, the marginal gains will be expressed in a big, positive impact on your wellness.

At the end of each experiment, you'll find a one-line takeaway to remind you of the key focus of the experiment – a talisman you can hold on to for the day if you choose.

TOXIC POSITIVITY

While this book is all about helping you to focus on your wellbeing and improve the quality and enjoyment of your life, it is most definitely NOT about being super-positive all the time. Forcing a smile, always looking on the bright side, feeling good vibes only, thinking positive always... when no space is allowed for "negative" emotions, that's toxic positivity.

Overwhelming positivity is toxic because it denies the reality of life: the struggle, the difficulties, the pain and heartbreak that is part and parcel of the human experience. Emotions are not negative or positive, they're simply emotions – they serve a purpose by giving us a message. Policing your feelings – minimizing how you feel, labelling emotions as good or bad, telling yourself what you should or should not feel – is not helpful; you need to allow your feelings to be, and move through them.

The experiment in this book that asks you to focus your attention on what's going well (Experiment 11, Keep a Gratitude Journal), for example, isn't asking you to deny what's not so great or to push away uncomfortable feelings; rather, for those ten minutes, it's simply asking you to give some of your energy to the good stuff in your life.

As you work your way through the experiments in this book, remember that all feelings that arise – good and bad – are welcome and allowed.

EXPERIMENTING IN YOUR OWN LIFE

You may be thinking it would be a whole lot easier if I just gave you a list of steps to follow or actions to carry out that would give you the results you want. Hmm, maybe. But what happens if some of the actions don't sit well with you or feel wrong for you? What if the action doesn't fit in with your life exactly as instructed? If I give you a map to follow and you take a wrong turn, or you can't actually take that turn, does that mean you've failed?

By avoiding a rigidly prescribed programme, we create space for exploration. You can be autonomous in deciding which experiments to try out (although I recommend you try them all, as you just never know…), in feeling what's right for you, and in adjusting the experiments to suit you and your life. Follow your gut.

Your you-ness

You are unique, as all humans are, and your life has its own special blend of challenges, responsibilities and dreams. There is no "one size fits all" way of living, so why would there be a one size fits all way to improve your wellbeing?

There are lots of things you can do to increase your resilience, your calm, your joy, to change your life for the better, many of which have been practised for thousands of years and/or thoroughly researched by esteemed clinicians and scientists. But just because a particular method or practice works for one person doesn't mean it will automatically work for you. If you've been told that a technique or strategy has been found to be beneficial and "Therefore, it will definitely benefit you" – and it doesn't, where does that leave you? A failure? Beyond help?

Certainly not. It just means that particular action, perhaps in that particular form, isn't a good fit for you. And there are plenty of other ideas that will be a great fit for you instead.

Not a get-out clause

I'm not suggesting you try an experiment in this book and if it feels a bit uncomfortable or odd or it doesn't instantly give you the results you want, you should conclude that it's not for you and toss it aside. This is not a get-out clause! Some of the actions *will* feel a bit uncomfortable or odd and won't instantly give you the results you want because they're new to you – it will take time for you to notice a difference (we're back to marginal gains).

But you do have a choice here. You're a grown-up and, "You have brains in your head. You have feet in your shoes. You can steer yourself any direction you choose," to quote Dr Seuss.[9]

LANGUAGE MATTERS

Using particular words or phrases is a tool that features in several experiments because it's a great way to give you focus. You may not realize it, but you already repeat (not necessarily helpful) mantras and affirmations to yourself, e.g., words and phrases like "Get on with it" or "Stupid", perhaps muttered under your breath or said silently in your head.

This language, repeated over and over, has an impact, because it's a message you're telling yourself again and again. And that impact can be unhelpful when you use it to criticize or berate yourself. Instead, throughout this book, I will encourage you to intentionally choose phrases or words to *support* yourself in how you want to feel and be, and what you want to do, not only in these experiments but in all aspects of your life.

You made the choice to pick up this book and start reading. You choose whether or not you give the experiments a go or continue with life as it is. You decide if you want to stick with an action as it is, tweak it and try again or move on to something else. You can choose to not read another page or to read but not put any of it into action – it's your choice, but let's also acknowledge that nothing will change if that's the case.

The next line in Dr Seuss's poem is, "You're on your own," but here you're not. You have this book to act as your guide. Within these pages, I'm here to suggest, to inspire, to motivate, to encourage and to cheerlead you on to taking just ten minutes a day to change your life for the better.

Making tweaks to how you live your life, starting new practices and habits, doing things differently, can feel risky because there's a lot at stake. And if you're of the perfectionist persuasion you will want to get it right, to make your life better; you won't want to mess up or get it wrong or miss a day because, in your mind, that will mean you've failed at improving your life.

That's a lot of pressure to pile on yourself!

Ease the pressure

This is why taking the experimental approach is so important – it takes off the pressure. When you experiment you try something out, you give it a go while being open to whatever the results could be. You're not expecting a specific result which, if it doesn't appear, means you've done it wrong.

Instead, with this book's guidance you can choose an experiment, give it a go, collect information on the experience and how it felt, and from there decide what to do next.

You might repeat it exactly; you may choose to change it a little (or a lot) and try again; or you may decide to set it aside and move on to another experiment.

Even though some of the actions I suggest may come with a wealth of evidence that positive results are found when it's carried out in a particular way, that doesn't mean that you can't tweak it and try it another way if you want – it's *your* experiment. You can choose to follow the method to the letter or freestyle it; you're a grown-up, you can make your own decisions!

Here's the thing about this book and experimenting in this way: I'm giving you the information, the inspiration and the evidence – but you have the autonomy to decide what to do with it. You're not being spoon-fed a prescriptive plan that you *must* follow to succeed. This is your life, the power is in your hands.

Forming habits

As you work through these experiments, you may find yourself creating rituals and forming habits (a ritual is an action such as meditating, a habit is the repeated performance of that action). There will be experiments that you choose to come back to over and over, to repeat on a regular, perhaps daily, basis because of how supportive you find them to your mental, emotional or physical wellbeing.

REGULATE YOUR NERVOUS SYSTEM

When you're stressed your sympathetic nervous system is activated and you go into fight or flight mode. Fight or flight can be activated by anything from a work deadline to an argument with your partner to jumping out of the way of a speeding car.

In fight or flight mode, your heart rate increases, your muscles tense, your breathing becomes quicker and shallower, and you act more on instinct than on measured thought. Your body releases hormones such as adrenaline and cortisol, which keep you in that stressed state.

A body that is experiencing stress and whose sympathetic nervous system is frequently activated is subject to wear and tear which, over time, takes a significant toll.

Meanwhile, the parasympathetic nervous system, known as the rest and digest system, is activated by feeling relaxed, safe and comfortable – for example when you're with people you like or you're doing something you enjoy. In this mode, your breathing and pulse rate slow and you physically feel more at ease.

We need to be moving through both states – fight or flight and rest and digest – to function well. However, modern living with all of its stresses can mean that we spend far more time in fight or flight than is good for our health.

Spending 1% of your day on these experiments will help you spend less time in an activated sympathetic nervous system state by lowering your stress levels and calming you.

Habits are built incrementally, one step at a time, one day at a time (Experiment 31 is specifically on forming a habit) through persistent and consistent repetition. And through these experiments and the individual habits you'll form, you'll also be building the overarching habit of taking better care of yourself.

Building self-trust

By making the choice (and it is a choice) to try these experiments, to commit to using 1% of your day to changing your life for the better, you will also build trust in yourself. You will be giving yourself the message that you are worth putting in the effort for, and demonstrating that you can show up for yourself by taking these steps.

Even if you try an experiment and decide it's not one you're going to pursue, you're still building your self-trust because *you* are making that decision for yourself – you're trusting that you know what's right for you.

And with greater self-trust comes a stronger belief that you can handle challenges and setbacks. You become kinder and more compassionate with yourself. You gain greater clarity and confidence in your decisions and actions.

INTRODUCTION

By working your way through these experiments, you'll learn a lot about yourself and come to understand yourself better, too. These actions will challenge you and will get you thinking about how you think and act. You'll also learn more about how external forces, including societal conditioning, have had a greater influence than you might have realized.

There is a *lot* of wellness information out there about all the things you *should* be doing; so much so, it can become quite bewildering to know what to do, when and how much. This book allows you to navigate your own path as you try out different tools and techniques – such as journaling, meditating or mindfulness – to discover what really works for you.

Through exploring the experiments, seeing what feels good for you, tweaking, and trying again, you'll create your own bespoke toolkit of practices. Some of what you take on will stay with you forever, others for seasons of your life – and all of them you will learn from.

HOW TO CONDUCT YOUR EXPERIMENTS

In this book there are 31 experiments, so you can conduct a month-long 1% Wellness Experiment. How you go about each experiment is up to you, and there are lots of options. Think about how you can make it easier on yourself to conduct these experiments and so reap the benefits from them.

When to experiment

You could choose to start on the first day of a new month or begin straight away. I personally advocate the "start right now" rather than the "start when your ducks are in a row/life's calmed down/the moon is in a particular house" approach, because it is too easy to put things off. You want to feel the benefit *now*, you want to make changes *now*, you want life to get good (to paraphrase Shania Twain) *now*, so why delay? If you're waiting for life to calm down, you could be waiting a long time, because life throws us curveballs all the time.

And let's remember we're only talking about using 1% of your day – ten minutes of your waking hours – that's all. There's no need to block out a chunk of your calendar or clear the decks first.

To give yourself the best possible chance of conducting an experiment a day, think about what could get in your way of finding the ten minutes each day. Even though it's a super short amount of time, if you know your day can run away from you as soon as you're out of bed, then you also know that your experiment could fall by the wayside until you remember you haven't done it and you're already collapsed, exhausted, in bed.

So, think about how you want to approach the experiments:

- Do you want to read the entire book to familiarize yourself first (just make sure that you do take action after reading)?
- Would you like to start your day reading an experiment and then choosing ten minutes during your day to carry it out?
- Do you fancy choosing and reading about an experiment the night before you conduct it the next day?
- Do you want to pick a specific time to experiment each day?

Which experiment to choose

Once you've decided when you're going to start, you can choose whether to follow the experiments as they're listed or pick one at random each day. There's no right or wrong way, it may be easier to follow the list, but dipping in and out is totally fine too. At the end of this chapter, you'll find a full list of experiments to help you keep track of what you've tried and how it went.

As I've said, and will keep saying, there's no wrong or right way to do this, the important thing is that you *do* do this. Follow your curiosity, be open to seeing where the experiment takes you and drop any expectation of what you think *should* happen or how it *should* go.

Keeping a record

Collecting data is an important part of conducting any experiment. By making a note of what happened, how you felt and what the outcome was, you can assess how the experiment went for you. It's not as black and white as success or failure; you're looking to see what it was like, the difference it made to you and what you can learn from the experience.

Here are some questions to help you reflect on your experience of each experiment:

- How did you feel before and after conducting the experiment?
- What worked well, and not so well?
- What did you enjoy, or not?
- What made it challenging and what could help make it easier?
- How could you adjust the action to work better for you?
- What did you learn about yourself through this experiment?
- What positive difference did the experiment make to you?
- Will you continue with this action?

You can jot down your answers to the questions, or just a few general notes on how it went for you, after each experiment so that you have them to look back on.

Depending on how it goes you may find:

- the experiment worked well and you want to repeat it in the same way
- it felt tricky or weird, but you want to try it again anyway
- you may want to tweak elements of the experiment to see what difference that makes
- it's something you have no desire to ever repeat again.

As I've said before, some of them will feel challenging because they're new or they go against the way you've done things for a long time. However, before you chuck out an experiment, I encourage you to take a moment to reflect on what's underneath your desire to ditch it. Then, if you still feel you have nothing to gain from it, let it go.

A clear benefit (in my view at least) of collecting data is that you need to store it somewhere – and that can mean new stationery! Any excuse to start a new notebook. You can just as easily write in the Notes app on your phone, record voice messages for yourself or film a video diary if that's what works for you.

By making a note, even roughly, of your experience of each experiment, you have this information to come back to. Through these notes, you will see which actions you want to keep repeating, what you find effective, and a record of your own tweaks and revisions of the experiments, so they're tailored to you. Gradually, day by day, you will be building your bespoke toolkit of powerful actions to support you well beyond the experimental month ending.

Missing a day

You have decided you're going to do an experiment a day for a month but at some point in those weeks you miss a day – work was manic, a family member was ill, the car broke down, a curveball of some kind came flying in or, you simply forgot.

No problem! Really, it's no problem if you miss a day, because missing a day is not what's important. What's important is what happens *next*.

You could get seriously cross with yourself, declare what you've done so far was a waste of time and give up because there's no point in carrying on – it's all ruined.

Or, and this is what I would much rather you do, you could acknowledge that you missed a day, give yourself a break because you're only human and that's what happens sometimes, and then recommit to *The 1% Wellness Experiment* once more.

Missing a day isn't important – *deciding to try again* is what's important. And that recommitment may happen over and over as days get missed here and there. That's okay, it's not a sign of weakness or flakiness or failure or anything else. You miss a day; you have another go.

For neatness, I'm suggesting you conduct an experiment a day for a month, but if it takes you much longer than that to try everything in this book, that's still a success because you've kept going. Doing the experiments "right" isn't the measure of success, just *doing them* is.

So, now you know the idea of marginal gains, the theory of experimenting, and how you're going to go about trying each of them, let's get practical and get experimenting!

Important note: *This book is not a substitute for professional medical advice. If you are experiencing mental, emotional or physical distress please seek help from a medical physician.*

KEEPING TRACK OF YOUR EXPERIMENTS

After each experiment tick a box to indicate if you loved it and want to repeat it or if the experiment needs a little tweak before trying again.

	Repeat!	Tweak & try again
1. Choose a guiding word	☐	☐
2. Be your own best friend	☐	☐
3. Make a mobile mood-boosting kit	☐	☐
4. Create a personal boundary	☐	☐
5. Conjure up your best future self	☐	☐
6. Take a deep breath	☐	☐
7. Perform random acts of kindness	☐	☐
8. Take control	☐	☐
9. Let your mind wander	☐	☐
10. Tidy your life	☐	☐
11. Keep a gratitude journal	☐	☐
12. Meditate	☐	☐
13. Say "no" (without feeling guilty)	☐	☐
14. Take a mindful walk	☐	☐
15. Make a morning ritual	☐	☐
16. Choose your cheerleading squad	☐	☐
17. Schedule "worry time"	☐	☐
18. Strengthen your connections	☐	☐

	Repeat!	Tweak & try again
19. Savour and delight	☐	☐
20. Uncover your inner strength	☐	☐
21. Have fun and play	☐	☐
22. Make a life wheel	☐	☐
23. Design a calm corner	☐	☐
24. Create your own positive affirmations	☐	☐
25. Do "future you" a favour	☐	☐
26. Create a sleep routine	☐	☐
27. End the day with a "Done" list	☐	☐
28. Put on your protective onesie	☐	☐
29. Give yourself permission	☐	☐
30. Try freestyle journaling	☐	☐
31. Make it a habit	☐	☐

EXPERIMENT 1

CHOOSE A GUIDING WORD

Let's get this experimental month off to a great start by creating a *positive intention*, or guiding word.

The idea behind choosing a guiding word is to give yourself a tool to remind you of how you want to feel, be or act. It's an anchor point that you can turn to at any time to bring you back to how you want to be operating in your life and the world.

Your guiding word is to be of service to you – to support, encourage and inspire you; to remind you of your values, of what's most important to you. It's not there to shame you, spark guilt or to be used as a stick to beat yourself with. Rather than be a goal that you strive for and achieve, your word is something you *journey with*, a state or emotion you want to embody.

Choosing a guiding word at the start of a calendar year is becoming a common practice, and a positive alternative to new year resolutions. However, picking a word to steer you doesn't need to only be an annual event – you can make use of this idea for any timeframe you like.

You can choose a guiding word for the day, week or month. Or for a project, a holiday or a season. It can relate to your self-development, your relationships with other people or your work. For example, as you embark on these experiments, why not choose a word to guide, inspire and motivate you for the month?

Let's look at some examples of guiding words.

- If you'd like to focus on taking better care of yourself, words such as "love", "nurture" or "compassion" might feel most supportive.
- If you have a big event at work that you're nervous about and you want to feel confident and capable, you might choose a word like "brave" or "poise".
- If you want to be intentional about creating more fun and joy in your life, you might choose a word like "delight", "laughter", "fun" or "joy".

YOUR WORD IS *YOUR* WORD

You can choose whatever word you like, it's *your* guiding word, not anyone else's. The only "rule" – let's call it a guideline – is that the word is what you really believe will be supportive to you.

It's not a word that you think you *should* have or one that you think will make you a better person in other people's eyes. You might have heard a buzzword that you think you *should* adopt, for example, "resilience", but consider whether that truly is the word that will best serve you. Do you feel like you *ought* to have that word but actually you don't really connect with it deep down? This is not a guiding word for other people (they can pick their own), this is for you. You don't have to tell anyone what your word is if you don't want to; although if accountability will help you to embody your word, telling a trusted friend could be helpful.

HOW TO CHOOSE YOUR WORD

So how do you go about choosing your word?

1. Begin by thinking of how you want to feel, how you want to be or how you want to behave during your specified timeframe. For example, if you're choosing a word for this

month of experimenting, you might want to feel nurtured, you might want to be mindful or taking action.

2. Write down all the words that come to mind on a piece of paper. Don't over-think it. So, continuing with our example above, those words could include "nurture", "mindful" or "action".

3. Now read through all the words you've written down and cross through any that don't really excite you, that you don't feel a connection with.

4. If you want to, check a thesaurus to see if it brings up different but similar words that strike more of a chord; add these to your list.

5. Repeat step 3.

6. Consider the words you have left – it's okay if there are still several words on the page.

7. Say each word out loud, one at a time, and notice if there's any kind of bodily reaction. That could feel like a flutter in your stomach, a sinking feeling, a warmth. This is your intuition, or gut instinct, helping you out by giving you a visceral reaction, and it's a good way to sidestep what word you might think you *should* be choosing. Any words that feel heavy, duty-bound or simply lacklustre will not serve you well, so cross them out.

8. Circle the words that evoke a good feeling – exciting, expansive or welcoming.

9. Take each word in turn and say it out loud again, this time imagining how you would feel if you embodied that word for this experimental month (or whatever timeframe you've chosen). Ask yourself:

   o   Does this word inspire me?
   o   Does this word motivate me?
   o   Does this word encourage me?
   o   Most importantly, does it feel supportive?
   o   When I bring this word to mind in the future, will I be thankful I have it as a reminder?

The word that answers "yes" most clearly to these questions is the guiding word for you.

Now you have chosen your guiding word, your reminder of how you want to feel and be as you explore this month of experiments.

USING YOUR GUIDING WORD

To keep your guiding word front and centre, try saying it to yourself at the start of each day, perhaps as you go about your morning routine. Or you could write it out at the top of your To Do list or diary page. Make it easy to remember by writing it on a note and keeping it in your wallet, making it the home screen image on your phone or drawing it out and sticking it on the fridge.

Notice how you feel after you've repeated your word to yourself a few times.

Every time you repeat your guiding word to yourself it will conjure up the feelings you want it to evoke; it will ground you and bring you back to what's important to you when you may be feeling unsure; it will remind you of your values, that *you* and your needs and desires are important.

And your guiding word will give you confidence in your intuition when you might be feeling self-doubt or swayed by what others are saying or doing.

If, later, you don't feel your chosen word is working for you, that's okay. Choose another word and try again, there are plenty of words to pick from, and this is an experiment after all!

TAKEAWAY

My guiding word is...

EXPERIMENT 2

BE YOUR OWN BEST FRIEND

Take a moment to consider how you talk to yourself – when you look in a mirror, when you're late, when you make a mistake, when you're procrastinating, when you're finding something difficult, when you're scared. We can be so quick to criticize, berate, chastise and be downright harsh with ourselves for the tiniest things. We treat ourselves so much more unkindly than we would ever treat someone we love, or even just like! So, for this ten-minute experiment you're going to work on being kinder to yourself.

WHY DOES IT MATTER?

You may think that if you're kind to yourself, if you don't crack the whip or give yourself a telling off, you'll become complacent, losing all motivation and ambition. You might believe your standards will slip – you'll become sloppy and nothing will get done.

But do you really believe that it's only by having a go at yourself, by chivvying yourself along, that you make any effort or accomplish anything in life? Really?

A verbal wake-up call can sometimes be the push you need, but if the voice inside your head is constantly mean and snarky, sneering and scornful, it can chip away at your self-worth, confidence and trust. This is because you're always listening. You hear everything you say to yourself, and say it over and over again and you'll soon believe it (check out Experiment 24, Create Your Own Positive Affirmations).

Maybe the first couple of times you criticize yourself it ignites a defiant "I'll show you" spirit; but, tell yourself enough times that you're useless at hitting deadlines, that you'll never be able to figure out the problem, that you're hopeless at making friends – whatever it is – and you'll have convinced yourself it's true.

If one of your closest friends spoke to you the way you talk to yourself, would you stand for it? And would you say the harsh and cruel things you say to yourself to someone you care about, love or respect?

A POWERFUL TOOL

There is a simple and incredibly powerful question I ask my coaching clients when they're struggling, when they're criticizing themselves and putting themselves down:

"If it was a good friend of yours in the same position as you're in, feeling the same way you do, what would you say to them?"

The answer nearly always comes quickly, and it's filled with compassion, kindness, empathy, understanding and encouragement.

It's much easier for us to think of how we'd help a friend who's finding something difficult, of how we would help them to see their good points, their strengths, to encourage them and build their confidence. So, when you've thought of what you'd say to a good friend in your position, flip that around and say it to yourself.

For example, you're nervous about going to an event where you know no one and will have to start conversations with strangers; the voice inside your head tells you, "Stop being so ridiculous. Don't be a wimp. Just talk to someone, and don't say anything stupid to embarrass yourself." Now imagine it's a friend in your position with the same anxieties; you might tell them, "It's okay to be nervous; lots of other people are bound to feel the same way." You'd remind your friend of similar situations they've been in before and how they coped, and you'd tell them, "I'm really proud of you that you're facing your fear and going to the event."

Flip those words around and apply them to yourself and you're going to feel a whole lot better about doing the scary thing than you would if you stuck with the snarky criticizing and self-flagellation.

THE BENEFITS OF SELF-COMPASSION

Essentially, what you're doing in this experiment is practising *self-compassion*. It's giving yourself the love and kindness that you give to other people.

Research has found that self-compassion brings with it a wealth of benefits.[1] People who are self-compassionate:

- experience less stress and anxiety, and are less likely to be depressed
- are more likely to feel fewer distressing emotions, such as fear and shame, and are also going to be less tangled up in them – not because they push them away but because they are kind and supportive to themselves when they feel them
- have higher levels of hope and vitality, as well as feeling happier and more content
- have increased resilience and ability to cope with challenges, as well as being more likely to take care of their health, (thus confounding the misconception that being kind to yourself will make you weak, unmotivated and self-indulgent)
- have better love lives as it helps them be more connected, accepting of and satisfied with their loved one without being a walkover, because they are more likely to compromise instead of completely giving up their own needs for their partner's.

What is not to like about self-compassion?!

THE THREE ELEMENTS OF SELF-COMPASSION

Kristin Neff, arguably the research queen of self-compassion, believes that self-compassion consists of three elements.[2]

1. **Self-kindness**. This involves understanding yourself, soothing and calming your troubled mind and comforting yourself with words and actions.
2. **Common humanity**. To practise self-compassion, you need to recognize that you're not alone in your suffering and your struggle. You might think you're the only one who finds something hard, but you never are. There will always be other people who struggle with the same things as you, however unique you may think it, and recognizing this helps you to feel less alone.
3. **Mindfulness**. This is being aware of what you're feeling, how you're talking to and treating yourself. You need to notice when you're suffering to be able to give yourself compassion.

So, just as in the example of being nervous about an event where you know no one, when you're compassionate with yourself you will:

- notice how you're feeling and what you're saying to yourself – mindfulness

- acknowledge that you're not the only one feeling that way – common humanity
- give yourself love, support and encouragement – self-kindness.

TRY IT TODAY

You have two options for practising self-compassion as your experiment for today:

a) Take ten minutes to think about a difficult occasion when you've been harsh and critical with yourself and replay it in your mind, changing the way you talk to yourself using the self-compassion elements listed above.
Here are some questions you might find helpful to think or write about:

- o On that occasion, how did you talk to yourself, what words did you use?
- o How did the occasion make you feel?
- o Can you imagine there are others who have felt like that?
- o If it was a good friend in your situation, what would you have said to them?
- o How would you have treated your friend?

- o Bearing that in mind, what could you have said to yourself?
- o How can you give yourself kindness, comfort and encouragement the next time you're struggling?

or

b) Throughout today, pay attention to the inner monologue inside your head; when you notice you're being unkind to yourself, pause and go through the elements of self-compassion to give yourself support and kindness instead.

Notice how you feel after you've given yourself some compassion, kindness and care. Don't be surprised if you notice you're unkind to yourself a *lot*. While you might wish you weren't so hard on yourself (and please don't get cross about getting cross with yourself!), it's a powerful realization, because now that you're more aware of it you can counter it more often with self-compassion.

TAKEAWAY

I treat myself like I'm my own best friend.

EXPERIMENT 3

MAKE A MOBILE
MOOD-BOOSTING KIT

Most of us are never far from our phones. There's even a term to describe the fear of being without your phone: "nomophobia", "nomo" being short for "no mobile phone".[1] Being glued to our phones can be unhelpful to our mental health, as work emails prevent us from switching off from our jobs, scrolling social media prompts FOMO (fear of missing out), and pinging alerts distract us from the joy of the present moment.

However, our phones aren't going anywhere, so let's make use of them to help our mental wellbeing. You can do that by creating your own bespoke mobile mood-boosting kit. This ten-minute experiment will get your kit up and running, and then you can add to it whenever you like.

HOW YOUR MOOD-BOOSTING KIT HELPS

Throughout a day, your mood can change dramatically depending on all kinds of factors: how much sleep you've had, what you've eaten or drunk, the weather, other people's words and actions, your workload, the news, etc. So it's useful to have a toolkit to hand that you can turn to any time you want to help yourself feel better.

The aim of this kit is to give you some support *in the moment*, when perhaps it's not possible for you to address your emotions on a deeper level – for example, when you've got an important meeting and you're feeling flat and lacking in confidence, or you're away from home missing your family and can't talk to them in that instance, or you're feeling frazzled from a day at work and need to deal with a houseful of children having a sleepover. It *isn't* for ignoring challenges in your life or covering up your feelings.

Because your phone is usually within reach, it means that you can access your kit any time you need or want it.

WHAT TO INCLUDE IN YOUR KIT

The beauty of this kit is that it is bespoke to *you*, and can include whatever *you* will find helpful, that can be stored on a phone. Here are several ideas for what you can include in your kit:

Music playlists

Whether you use iTunes, Spotify or another streaming service, you can create multiple playlists, one for every mood you want to address. Research shows that listening to music can lower feelings of tiredness, sadness and fear, can boost your happiness and wellbeing, and is an effective tool in stressful times.[2]

Here are some playlist suggestions:

- Calming playlist – soothing classical tunes or ambient tracks to relax you.
- Energizing playlist – upbeat, fast tempo songs to get your blood pumping and raise your energy levels.
- Empowering playlist – songs with strong lyrics to boost your confidence and determination.

Meditation app

When you're in need of calm, grounding comfort, listening to a guided meditation could be exactly what you need. Download an app (many are free, see Experiment 12,

Meditate) and save or bookmark your favourites. Choose a variety, based on their duration and focus – for example, reducing anxiety, dealing with change, having more self-compassion – so that you can choose the meditation you need in the moment you need it.

Video playlist

What is the internet good for if not watching videos of puppies, kittens and babies being cute and funny? YouTube has approximately a bajillion videos of whatever makes you giggle, from puppies trying to climb stairs to your favourite comedians doing stand-up. Make a playlist of funnies that you can quickly turn to and watch any time you need to be tickled.

Photo album

If your phone is anything like mine, you'll have thousands of photos taken over several years and none of which you've printed! Make yourself a handy digital photo album you can carry with you at all times of everyone and everything you love. Save photos of your beloved family and friends, your adored pets, treasured holiday snaps – any pictures that make you feel good to gaze upon – into an album on your phone and give it a memorable (or funny) name so you can easily find it.

Voice memos

Sometimes, when you're having a wobble or a low moment, what you need to hear more than anything else is the voice of a loved one. Ask someone special to you to record a message, or several, with words of comfort, encouragement or advice, as a voice note on your phone so it's there ready for you to listen to when you can't speak with them directly. You could even record voice notes to yourself (I know listening to your own voice can be weird, but give it a go) so that future you can hear a message from past you.

Affirmations

Reading powerful, positive statements to counteract the doubting, unsupportive words you're saying to yourself can bring about a real shift in your mood. So, as a list in your Notes app or perhaps a photo album of images saved from social media, create a bank of affirmations that will help you to strengthen the beliefs you want and boost your mood (see Experiment 24, Create Your Own Positive Affirmations).

Action list

When you're feeling in a funk, it can be hard to think of what to do to shift yourself out of it. Help future fed-up you by writing a list today of all the actions you can take (aside from the rest of your kit) to get out of the grumps and into a better mood. With this list in hand, you won't have to try and think what to do in the moment; you can just bring up the action list on your phone, choose something to do that the situation allows, and off you go.

Your action list could include:

- Go for a walk
- Phone a friend
- Do some mindful colouring
- Put on your favourite top
- Take five deep breaths in and out
- Scream into a pillow
- Eat something tasty
- Put on make-up
- Do five star jumps
- Write in your journal

You can even divide your list by duration (e.g. 5 minutes, an hour, half a day) so that you can easily see what's doable in the time you have at that moment.

Whatever you want in your kit is up to you. It doesn't matter if it's different to what someone else would have in their kit, because it's *your* mobile mood-boosting kit made specifically for *you*.

TAKEAWAY

My mood-boosters are always within reach.

EXPERIMENT 4

CREATE A PERSONAL BOUNDARY

Personal boundaries are integral to our wellbeing, but they can feel confusing, difficult and sometimes mean-spirited when you don't understand them. They're also a *big* topic, one that entire books are written about. For this experiment, we're going to focus on creating, communicating and honouring *one* boundary.

WHAT IS A PERSONAL BOUNDARY?

The American Psychological Association's definition of a boundary is, "a psychological demarcation that protects the integrity of an individual or group or that helps the person or group set realistic limits on participation in a relationship or activity".[1] In other words, boundaries are an expression of what we want and need in a relationship, of what is and is not okay with us, whether it's in relation to a person, an organization or even technology.

BOUNDARIES CAN BE RIGID OR LEAKY

Boundaries are often thought of as walls to keep people out – strict lines that have to be defended and if anyone dares cross them, we have to come down hard. However, rigid boundaries prevent you getting close to other people or asking for help because you're keeping everyone at arm's length.

At the other extreme there are "porous"[2] or leaky boundaries. This is where you find it really difficult to say "No" (see Experiment 13, Say "No" (Without Feeling Guilty)), and as a result put up with being treated badly. Leaky boundaries can also leave you feeling responsible for other people's happiness and wellbeing, and lead you to getting involved in trying to "fix" others and/or their problems.

HOW TO RECOGNIZE HEALTHY BOUNDARIES

What we're aiming for is *healthy* boundaries, because they make for healthy relationships. This is where you not only know your own needs, wants and views, you also value and respect your right to them. You communicate these boundaries to others, and you are respectful and accepting of other people's boundaries as well. Boundaries are about doing what's best for us, not about controlling another person's behaviour.

BOUNDARIES ARE YOUR VALUES IN ACTION

If one of your core values is, for example, kindness, to honour that value requires you to be kind not only to others but to yourself as well.

If you allow someone else to be unkind to you (whether they're doing it intentionally or not), because you think that's the "kind" thing for you to do, it isn't really being kind at all, and you're not honouring what you stand for or what's of core importance to you.

Healthy boundaries are kind, clear and respectful

When we aren't clear on what our boundaries are, when we don't communicate them or honour our own boundaries, it can lead to confusion, resentment or upset among those around us. When we're clear about what we want and need, about what is and is not okay with us, other people know where they stand too.

Say, for example, you're asked to do something you don't want to do or don't have time for. However, you feel awkward about turning it down because you think it's wrong of you to deny any request made of you, so you agree to it. And then you try to get out of it, or you cancel last minute, or you do it unhappily with resentment or discomfort leaking out of you.

This can be pretty confusing for the other person, and it isn't really kind to them (or you). Even though wanting to be kind (or thought of as kind) is what drove you to agree in the first place, your initial words don't end up matching your behaviour. Even if you manage to hide your resentment, *you* know how you feel. There's a dishonesty in knowing you're not giving your time or energy freely and pretending otherwise.

However, by turning the request down with compassion and kindness you show respect for the other person, and for yourself, by communicating clearly. There's no confusion or misunderstanding, and everyone knows where they stand. That doesn't mean that it won't feel uncomfortable or you won't get pushback (you may not!). It can be challenging to honour your boundaries and communicate them when you're not used to doing it.

SHOW AS WELL AS TELL

When you've been that person with wishy-washy, porous boundaries, the people around you are used to you going along with what they want or dropping everything to help them.

When you don't honour your own boundaries, other people don't think you're serious – so why would they take your so-called boundaries seriously?

When you begin to speak up for what *you* want or need, when you don't go along with them or jump when they call, that may be surprising for them. However, when you honour your own boundaries, others learn to honour them as well. We teach people how to treat us by honouring our own boundaries.

For example, if you tell a friend that you don't like to take phone calls after 8pm (perhaps this is to help you wind down for bed), but whenever they call after 8pm you always answer, you're not honouring your own boundary. This indicates to the other person that you didn't really mean what you said, so they can call you any time and their expectation is that you'll answer. Whereas if you didn't pick up the phone, they'd quickly learn that you were serious about this boundary. (Note that you're not telling your friend they're not allowed to call you – you're not trying to control their behaviour. You're simply saying that if they do call you won't answer because you don't answer after a specific time.)

(If you're worried about missing an emergency, you can always give the caveat that if it's urgent your friend can leave a voicemail or send a text telling you what the emergency is. This way you can listen or read and choose what you want to do next.)

CREATE BOUNDARIES

For this experiment you're going to take ten minutes to come up with one (or more) boundary, and put it into action at some point during the day.

1. First choose an area of your life you'd like to create a boundary for.

   o Personal relationships
   o Work relationships
   o Your relationship with technology (e.g. digital device use, social media scrolling, computer gaming)

2. Next think about the boundary you want to create, it may help to consider the following questions.

   o Think of a situation where you felt hurt, resentful or uncomfortable – what specifically prompted those feelings?

o What do you frequently do even though you don't
   want to?
o What do you want or need to do?
o What do you want or need to feel?
o What do you wish you could ask other people to
   respect about you?

Here are some examples:

o *When I offload, my partner tries to find solutions when
   I just want him to listen.*
o *I hate replying to emails on weekends, but I'm worried
   clients expect me to.*
o *It really upsets me that my friend interrupts me when
   I'm talking, but I just let her.*
o *I want to enjoy just being with my family at the dinner
   table instead of our phones distracting us.*
o *I need a break during the day where I can just be left
   alone for a while!*

3. Craft your wish into a statement so you're clear what it is
   you want and need. For example:

o *I want to feel listened to and supported, not fixed.*
o *I will only respond to emails during my working hours.*

- *I want my voice to be heard.*
- *Mealtimes are a device-free zone.*
- *I need to go for lunchtime walks on my own.*

4. Now you've defined your boundary to yourself you need to put it into action by communicating it with the outside world. This could look like:

- Telling your partner: *When I'm letting off steam, I need you to just listen to me. If I want help finding a solution I'll let you know.*
- Setting up an email auto-responder with the message: *My working hours are 9am to 5pm, Monday to Friday, and I reply to emails during these hours. If your email arrives outside of these times I will respond on my next working day.*
- Saying to your friend when she next interrupts you: *Hang on, I'm not finished yet.*
- Letting your family know that devices are not welcome at the table and to leave them outside the room at mealtimes.
- Blocking out time in the middle of the day on your work calendar and telling any colleagues who ask to speak to you then that you take solo lunchtime walks to recharge.

Remember, if you're new to creating, communicating and honouring boundaries this may feel uncomfortable. Be kind to yourself and experiment with one boundary to begin with – you can build up from there. You may get pushback, but know that:

- you're allowed to have boundaries
- boundaries support healthy relationships
- by being clear about your boundaries there's no confusion or misunderstanding
- by upholding your own boundaries other people will learn to respect them.

So, first identify and create a boundary, then put it into action by communicating and honouring it, and see how you get on

TAKEAWAY

Boundaries are kind, clear and respectful, for me and for others.

EXPERIMENT 5

CONJURE UP YOUR BEST FUTURE SELF

Have you ever daydreamed about a life in the future where you've met your goals, achieved what you wanted and you're living your best life?

If you have, you'll know what a warm, fuzzy glow you can get from allowing your imagination to travel forward in time to this vision of a content and fulfilled life. What you may not know is that this kind of future thinking has been shown to boost your mood and increase your optimism.

Research by the University of California[1] found that writing about your best possible future self (an action inspired by solution-focused therapy), results in an immediate boost to your mood; and if you continue to repeat this exercise over the weeks you can continue to reap the positive benefits.

HARNESS YOUR IMAGINATION

So, for this experiment we're going to harness your imagination. Choose a calm ten-minute gap in your day, when you're not rushing from one thing to the next, and you can truly give yourself over to this exercise. Perhaps make a cup of tea, put your phone on silent, switch off email and tell anyone around you that you're unavailable for the next ten minutes.

In that time, you're going to write (we'll come on to why it's important to write and not just think) about your best possible future self. You can choose the timeframe – five, ten, twenty years' time. You need to imagine a life where you've worked hard to achieve your goals, you're living true to your values, you're fulfilled, happy and all is as good as you imagine it can be.

As you write, let yourself really step into your best possible future self. What does your life look like?

- Who is with you? Are you alone, with a partner, or with family?
- Where are you? Are you in a particular part of the world? What is your home like?
- What are you doing? Imagine the work you've done or are doing, the goals you've accomplished
- How do you feel – satisfied and rewarded?

WHY WRITE?

There's a reason that writing Is preferable, if possible, to just thinking about your vision of life. Put simply, writing takes longer than thinking. You're organizing and analysing your thoughts as you write them into sentences. Having your words written down makes it possible to read them back, to reflect on what you've imagined as your best possible future self.

If writing is not available to you, please don't let that stop you from experimenting with this exercise. You'll still gain from taking ten minutes to talk through your best possible future self out loud rather than to not do it at all. You may find it helpful to record a voice note on your phone as you talk; you can then play it back and reflect on the life you're imagining.

ANALYSE YOUR VISION

Once you've written about your best self, take time to read it through.

This exercise isn't about fooling yourself with an outlandish and unachievable fantasy. It's about allowing yourself to focus on what's important to you, what matters, what lights you up, what you want to achieve and who you really are.

You may find that your best possible future self isn't wildly different from who you are now; that what you visualize for your future isn't out of reach – it's attainable and you can see the beginnings of a path to get there.

You may see themes develop or discover goals that you hadn't realized are so important to you. You may surprise yourself by writing about something that you hadn't given much time to before, and through this process uncover a desire you want to explore further.

By taking even this short amount of time to imagine life as your best possible future self, you are gaining clarity on what you want in life, which makes it more likely you'll take steps to make it a reality.

TAKING IT FURTHER

If you want to take this experiment beyond 1% of your day, you may like to follow a study undertaken by the University of Missouri-Columbia[2] where participants were asked to write about their best possible future selves for 20 minutes a day on four consecutive days. Those researchers found this resulted in a significant increase in positive mood and optimism, and participants even reported feeling ill less often months later!

As with all these experiments, try it out for ten minutes and see how it goes. Perhaps you will choose to write about your best possible future self again or read over what you've written over the coming days, or maybe you will decide to move on to the next experiment. As always, it's up to you.

TAKEAWAY

My best possible future self is within my grasp.

EXPERIMENT 6

TAKE A DEEP BREATH

You know how to breathe, you've been doing it your whole life. However, when we get stressed, we take shallow breaths, and don't use the full capacity of our lungs. In fact, at times throughout the day you may even be holding your breath for no other reason than you're concentrating on a task! There's even a name for holding your breath when you're reading emails or looking at a screen (which you may well do without realizing) – "screen apnea".[1] We can actually forget to breathe.

So, today we're experimenting with how your breath affects how you feel.

SHORT, SHALLOW BREATHS INDUCE STRESS HORMONES

Restricting your breathing (not breathing fully into your diaphragm) indicates to your brain and body that something's wrong, that you're in danger and you need to be on high alert. Your sympathetic nervous system is activated and you go into fight or flight mode. In this activated mode, your body releases hormones such as adrenaline and cortisol, which create more stress and on the cycle goes.[2]

This automatic response is a hangover from the days when we were in danger of being eaten by tigers and bears, but now it can be triggered by a traffic jam, an email, an offhand comment or a social media post. We may not be consciously aware of what exactly is going on – perhaps we just feel a bit tense, short of breath or have a headache – but inside it's all kicking off. A body that is experiencing stress and whose sympathetic nervous system is frequently activated is subject to wear and tear, which, over time, takes a significant toll.

SLOW AND STEADY CALMS YOUR NERVOUS SYSTEM

Taking a few deep, slow breaths is a powerful way to combat this powerful nervous system response, and to reduce its reoccurrence.

When you breathe in slowly and deeply you take in more oxygen which increases the oxygen level in your blood, more than if you're breathing shallowly or irregularly.[3] Exhaling slowly activates your parasympathetic nervous system, your "rest and digest" mode, which tells your brain and body that you're okay and you can come off high alert.

Research in China where participants went through an eight-week training programme, found that deep and slow breathing (known as diaphragmatic breathing) significantly lowered anxiety levels and reduced heart rate.[4]

YOUR BREATHING TODAY

Try this experiment right now to see for yourself, as well as any time you notice you're getting tense and stressed (or you've been staring at a screen for a while).

It won't even take 1% of your day (and it may be the only time in the day when you breathe fully), as you're going to take just ten slow, deep, intentional breaths.

Before you begin you might want to take note of how you feel mentally and physically so that you can compare how you feel afterwards. Are there any areas of your body that feel tense? What thoughts are you having?

1. Begin by slowly breathing in through your nose, if possible. (The advantage of breathing through your nose

is that it filters out dust and particles, warms or cools the air and helps more oxygen get into your blood.) You don't need to count, it's whatever slow means for you without forcing it. Try to visualize pulling the air down to the bottom of your torso so that your tummy expands.

2. Then, as you slowly exhale (through your mouth or nose) let your tummy contract and imagine expelling the air from your body. You'll probably find that your exhale is naturally longer than your inhale. Exhaling fully is as important as inhaling fully – gulping in air without breathing it out can make you feel light-headed.

3. Breathe in slowly again, pulling the air deep into your body. And breathe out slowly, letting the air flow back out.

4. Continue doing this – breathing in and out, slowly and deeply – for another eight breaths so you take ten intentional breaths in total.

Now you have taken ten intentional breaths, how do you feel? And how does that compare to what you noted before you began this experiment?

SOOTHE YOUR BODY AND BRAIN

If you notice you're feeling calmer and your body feels more relaxed, it may not be just because of the intentional breathing. This experiment provides a double whammy.

The act of paying attention to your breath, noticing your stomach and chest rise and fall requires your full focus. This focus gives your brain a break from whatever was occupying it before. Focus is one of the foundations of mindfulness, anchoring you to the present moment.

Focusing your attention on a different, "neutral" matter instead of the many thoughts whizzing through your brain, along with the deeper, slower breathing, helps to calm and soothe your body and brain.

The handy thing about this experiment is that you can do it anytime, anywhere and no one need know you're doing it. You can take ten (or fewer, or more) deep slow breaths at your desk, in a meeting, on a crowded bus, in the supermarket queue, while making dinner... whenever you want to bring down your stress level and feel calmer and in control.

TAKEAWAY

Breathe in, breathe out.

EXPERIMENT 7

PERFORM RANDOM ACTS OF KINDNESS

You may be already familiar with the term "random acts of kindness", which has even had a dedicated day (17 February) in the calendar since the 1990s.

A random act of kindness (aka RAK) is doing something for someone else without expecting to be rewarded for it. The "random" element is that it can be spontaneous, but it doesn't have to be. And RAKs are the focus of today's 1% experiment!

Acts of kindness can vary enormously. Here are a few examples:

- Letting someone in ahead of you in a queue.
- Writing a celebratory or encouraging comment on a social media post.
- Donating blood.

- Shovelling snow from your neighbour's path.
- Volunteering for a litter pick.
- Giving a compliment.

The examples I've given don't cost any money. However, it has been found that spending money on other people, rather than yourself, can also increase your own happiness. Interestingly, the *amount* of money doesn't make a difference. Research found that whether you spend £20 or £5 on someone else, the effect on your happiness level is the same.[1]

The important point with a random act of kindness is that you're doing something of value for someone else, with no expectation of thanks or reward, just because you can and because it's a good thing to do.

THE MANY BENEFITS OF KIND ACTS

You'd think that it's the person on the receiving end of the act of kindness who benefits, wouldn't you? And they do, but they're not the only one. You, the person carrying out the act of kindness, as well as anyone in the vicinity who simply observes the kind act, benefit too.

A study in the US asked groups of participants to perform between three and nine acts of kindness a week for ten weeks.[2] Some repeated the same acts, while others varied them. The study found that increasing the number of acts from three a week to nine didn't have a lasting effect on happiness, but performing a *variety* of kind acts, rather than repeating the same one, increased happiness levels (which remained elevated a month later).

Another study, this time in Japan, looked at the impact of becoming more *aware* of the kind acts performed by asking participants to write down the number of acts of kindness they carried out each day for a week. The researchers found that simply counting how many kind acts they'd performed each day increased how happy the participants felt by the end of the week.[3] So, while a truly altruistic act is done with zero expectation of reward, you will inevitably gain from your actions.

As mentioned, the benefits of RAKs stretch beyond those directly involved in them. Simply seeing, hearing or reading about an altruistic act has been found to spur on people to commit their own generous and thoughtful deeds.[4] This means that the kind thing you do could create a ripple effect of more kind acts by more people that you don't even know about!

GET ACTING

Your experiment today is to spend ten minutes carrying out acts of kindness, random or not. Try to vary rather than repeat the same ones, and remember to drop any thoughts of being thanked or rewarded, or any expectation of it to be reciprocated. You're doing this purely with the intention of putting kindness out into the world.

Here are 20 ideas to get you going:

1. Hold a door open for a stranger.
2. Give a neighbour a posy of flowers (bought or from your garden).
3. Buy a coffee for the person behind you in the coffee shop queue.
4. Give a book you enjoyed to a friend you think will appreciate it too.
5. Compliment a shop owner on their window display.
6. Give money to charity.
7. Reply to a newsletter you enjoyed to thank the writer.
8. Wash your partner's car.
9. Offer to do the grocery shopping for an elderly neighbour.
10. Take cake into work for your colleagues.

11. Send a text to tell your friend how much you value them.
12. Donate clothes and books to charity.
13. Send a handwritten card to a friend or relative to let them know you're thinking of them.
14. Drop off a box of biscuits at your local hospital for the staff.
15. Post about your favourite independent shop on social media.
16. Compliment a colleague on their work.
17. Give your seat on a train or bus to someone else.
18. Put items in a food bank collection box.
19. Write a glowing review for a pub, restaurant or hotel you've enjoyed.
20. Offer to babysit or dog-sit for a friend or neighbour.

Take note of how you feel before your kind acts and what you notice has changed afterwards. Also note down how many and what kind of acts you carried out. Which acts did you particularly enjoy? What response, if any, from others did you get?

TAKEAWAY

I spread kindness wherever I go.

EXPERIMENT 8

TAKE CONTROL

There's a lot in life that is uncertain, unknown, out of our control and we just can't get a firm grip on it. For some people that's okay, they don't mind there being question marks over much of life. For others, however, uncertainty is a great source of stress. Not knowing what's going to happen next, or where, when, why or how, can press your anxiety buttons and cause you to spend a significant amount of time trying to control what may be, ultimately, uncontrollable.

Some things in life that are uncertain and may be a source of stress might seem quite small; for example, not knowing what time a party is going to end or how busy the traffic will be. Other uncertainties feel bigger and riskier, such as how secure your position at work is or how much your broken-down car will cost to fix.

Then there's the stuff in life where we *know* we don't have ultimate control, and so think we can't exert much or perhaps any power over it, where we feel powerless to make a significant difference. Yet knowing we have little influence over something doesn't necessarily stop us from fretting and wishing we *could* do something – for example, an earthquake in a faraway country, changes in government policy, or climate change.

We can feel small, helpless, frustrated and insignificant in the face of such challenges. All of which feels pretty horrible!

Whether it's something on the global stage or a detail in your own life, you can spend a lot of brain power, time and energy on worrying about what *could* happen – the potential consequences – and wishing you had some control over what you, ultimately, don't have control over.

For this experiment, we're going to try an exercise that is a quick and powerful way to counteract the feeling that everything is out of your control.

CONTROL, INFLUENCE, ACCEPT

The Control, Influence, Accept exercise is inspired by American educator Stephen Covey's circles of concern and influence.[1]

To identify and understand what *is* within your control we need to also identify what is in your sphere of influence and what is outside of your control.

What you need
- A piece of paper and a pen or pencil.
- An example of something you don't feel you have control over that's stressing you out.

What to do
Draw three circles on the piece of paper, one inside the other, so it looks like a fried egg in the centre of a plate.

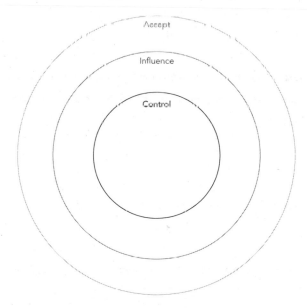

Label the centre circle **Control**, label the middle ring **Influence** and label the outer circle **Accept**.

Before using this for your particular challenging issue, let's look at how it works with an example.

Another country's leader has invaded a nation and the ensuing war is causing death and devastation; you feel powerless as you watch it reported on the news.

Step 1: *Accept* what is out of your control

Identify what is definitely out of your control and/or who is not under your control, and write this in the outer Accept circle.

Everything you list here you can't do anything about, so to continue to wish and strive to change it, when it's not possible, is using up your valuable time and energy and keeping you stuck in stress.

Accept it, however hard that feels, and move on.

In our example of the war, what is out of your control is:

- Stopping the invading leader – you can't physically make them change their mind or behaviour.

- How the invaded country reacts and responds.
- How the war is reported in the news.

All of this, everything that's not within your power to change, goes in the Accept circle.

Step 2: What you can *influence*

Consider what you can do to influence the situation and/or who could come under your sphere of influence; that is, what or who is not completely out of your control or completely within your control, but on which or whom you may be able to exert some influence. Write your findings down in the middle Influence circle.

These findings are the actions you can take and, once you've done so, know that's as far as you can take it. You can exert influence but you cannot control; use your time and efforts to take the steps you've identified, and then let it go.

In our example, you can try and influence by:

- Writing to your MP to tell them how you feel about the invasion and ensuing humanitarian crisis, and what action you want the government to take. You can't make your MP do anything but you can try to influence them.

- Sharing social media posts by the charities working to help the people in need.
- Talking to friends and family about the crisis and let them know how they can donate to the relief efforts.

Remember, you can try to influence people by sharing information, but you can't actually make them do anything with the knowledge you've imparted, however passionate and emphatic you are.

Step 3: What is within your *control*

In the centre circle focus on what *is* within your control – this is what you *can* do and what you *do* have power over. Your own actions, words, attitude and approach are always within your control – how you choose to respond, and what you choose to say or do. You have much more control over what you do with your time, your energy, your words, your belongings, than you do over anyone else, and this is what goes in the centre Control circle.

What's written in the Control circle is where best to focus your time, thoughts, power and energy, because this is where you can have an impact, this is where you can make a difference, this is where your power lies – in what you do and say.

In our example, what is within your control is:

- Making the choice to contact your MP.
- Sharing information online and in person.
- Donating money to the charities working on the ground, or donating your time to raise awareness and funds for them.
- Finding out what's happening with refugees fleeing the war and coming to your country and how you can support them.
- Looking at the bigger picture so you're not just focusing on what you can or can't do with this specific crisis, but at what you can do to make a difference to other people experiencing hardship, loss and suffering elsewhere and in your own community.
- Contacting organizations working in your local area, for example, food banks, refugee and homeless charities, to find out how you can provide support through donating time, money, and perhaps items like food or clothes, as well as raising awareness.

Your three circles will end up looking something like this:

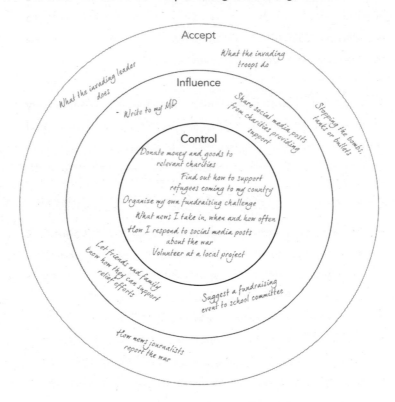

Accept

What the invading
troops do

What the invading leader
does

Influence

- Write to my MP

Share social media posts
from charities providing
support

Stopping the bombs,
tanks or bullets

Control

Donate money and goods to
relevant charities

Find out how to support
refugees coming to my country

Organize my own fundraising challenge

What news I take in, when and how often

How I respond to social media posts
about the war

Volunteer at a local project

Let friends and family
know how they can support
relief efforts

Suggest a fundraising
event to school committee

How news journalists
report the war

The focus of your attention

It's the centre circle, the place where you focus on what is within your control, that often has the most written in it. This is because we have more power than we may at first think.

Using our example, you can go from feeling desperate sadness and helplessness at the awful situation in a country far away, to realizing you have the power to take action to make a difference to other people's lives straight away.

And this applies to everything in life, to small everyday occurrences, and not just to crises happening on the global stage.

WHAT YOU DO AND DON'T CONTROL

- You don't have control over someone gossiping about your colleagues in the office kitchen, but you *do* have control over whether or not you join in, give another side to the story, tell the people being talked about. You have control over what you say and do.
- You don't have control over what's reported in the news, but you *do* have control over how you access the news – whether you watch it on TV, listen to the radio, read newspapers, find it online. You choose how often you consume news – whether you check in every hour, twice a day or have news alerts on your phone – and at what time of day – is watching the news straight before bed conducive to a good night's sleep?

- You have no say over what someone else posts on social media, but you *do* control who you follow, how often you open the app, how long you scroll for and how you respond to the posts you see.
- You don't have power over the weather, but you *do* get to decide what to wear, whether to carry an umbrella or not and on your attitude to an unexpected downpour.
- Ultimately, and this can be the most frustrating, you can't control other people – but you *can* control how you respond to them.

APPLY CONTROL, INFLUENCE, ACCEPT TO YOUR LIFE

Now think of something you don't feel you have control over that's stressing you out and take ten minutes to go through the Control, Influence, Accept exercise.

See what difference it makes to how you feel about someone or something that is feeling stressful because you don't believe you have any control.

For recurring challenges, you may find it helpful to keep hold of the piece of paper you've used to complete the exercise on. This way, the next time you find yourself feeling anxious or stressed over the same issue, you can pull out the diagram and remind yourself of what's within your control and so where to direct your time, energy and brain power.

TAKEAWAY

I control what I can and let go of what I can't.

EXPERIMENT 9

LET YOUR MIND WANDER

This experiment may be the simplest one of all... and the hardest... and the most beneficial... and the most challenging.

Because for ten minutes I want you to experiment with doing... absolutely nothing. Don't do or think about anything in particular.

You don't have to meditate, or write a list, or focus on your breathing, or tune into your senses, or repeat an affirmation, or listen to music, or read...

Just let your mind wander.

YIKES!

The thought of doing nothing for ten minutes may be making you feel panicky. How can you do nothing?! You've too much to do – it's selfish and lazy and wrong to be idle for ten whole minutes – just think what you could get done in that time!

Is it selfish and lazy and wrong – really? Or have we just learned over our lifetimes that we *should* be busy and productive, and to do otherwise is lazy and selfish and wrong?

Before we had the world encapsulated in the phone in our pocket, if we were in a queue or waiting room without a book or a Walkman (remember them?!), we had no choice but to just be – with our thoughts. But we're out of that habit because, thanks to the wonders of technology, we can *always* find something to occupy our minds, which means our brains never get the chance to wander freely.

Now, how often do you take ten minutes to just "be"? Without making lists or planning (in your head or written down), without rehearsing or dissecting conversations, without scrolling on your phone, listening to the radio or zoning out in front of the TV? Without willing yourself to fall asleep?

When did you last allow your brain to amble and drift?

You're not trying to empty your head or stop yourself from thinking. For these ten minutes you can let your mind wander wherever it wants to. It's actually quite fascinating to notice the variety and volume of random thoughts that pop into your head when you allow it free rein!

WHAT YOU CAN GAIN

There can be a fear stopping us from letting our minds drift – a fear that we'll have thoughts and feelings that will be unwanted or uncomfortable, and which we won't know what to do with or will perhaps struggle to handle. However, these fears may be unjustified. A study carried out in Japan and the UK in 2022 that asked people to sit in a quiet room without any books, music or phones and just think, for up to 20 minutes, found participants enjoyed the experience more than they thought they would.[1]

There are benefits to be found in allowing your mind to meander: research suggests that mind-wandering enhances creativity and problem-solving.[2]

Even without the research, we know in our hearts and our guts that taking a break, giving ourselves a moment to catch our breath and hop off the mad merry-go-round that is ordinary life, for just ten minutes is going to help. A brief respite where we're not in demand and we're not demanding anything of ourselves is like pressing a reset button.

So, set a timer for ten minutes, sit, stand or lie down, and just let your mind wander...

TAKEAWAY

I'm free to let my mind wander.

EXPERIMENT 10

TIDY YOUR LIFE

You know that feeling you get from knowing there are boring, tedious jobs that need doing but you just don't want to do them? They hang around you like a bad smell. They follow you around and pull at your sleeve. They sit on your shoulder and nag in your ear.

This is life admin.

WHAT ARE LIFE ADMIN TASKS?

Here are a few examples of what life admin can look like:

- Booking a health appointment – sight test, hearing test, medical check-up, smear test.
- Booking a car MOT or service.
- Renewing the TV licence.

- Comparing or renewing insurance – house, car, holiday, health.
- Paying a credit card bill.
- Paying fees – gym, school, membership.
- Cancelling unwanted subscriptions – magazines, streaming services.
- Unsubscribing from unwanted email newsletters.
- Completing an application form – passport, job, education, membership.
- Filing paperwork.

Life admin often consists of the dull, necessary tasks that are part of adulthood, but don't hold any of the fun we thought being a grown-up would involve. None of us grew up yearning for the day we would be old enough to book a mammogram or compare mortgage rates.

These jobs can involve hunting for emails or paperwork that didn't get filed away neatly (a life admin task in itself), and so could be hiding anywhere on your computer or in your home; doing maths (not my strong suit, how about you?); or making phone calls (and waiting on hold).

However, this not-so-thrilling stuff of life doesn't go away. In fact, ignoring it can make it worse. While you know you're going to have to get around to addressing it sometime, you put it off and it continues to niggle at you. Another thing to berate yourself for not doing or remembering. Which is why today's experiment is focused on taking ten minutes to tidy up your life admin.

Once you've done what needed doing, once you've ticked those tedious jobs off the list, you'll be rewarded with the feelings of satisfaction and accomplishment! The reward may not be tangible, but the relief of knowing it's done and dusted and off your plate is very real. The millstone is no longer around your neck, you don't have to hold it in your memory any longer and you've freed up space in your mind and your day – as even little tasks that can be completed in a minute have the power to take up your time, energy and brainpower in just thinking about having to do them.

WHAT ABOUT THE TIME IT TAKES TO *DO* THE LIFE ADMIN?

We often think that whatever the life admin task is, it's going to require a big investment of our time and energy, which is what puts us off actually doing it.

This is where our 1% experiment comes in – you're only going to spend ten minutes on life admin today. And however far you get, whatever progress you make in ten minutes, that will have moved you on further than if you hadn't spent any time at all.

CHOOSE YOUR LIFE ADMIN TASK

Deciding what to do could take up much of your precious time if you let it, so don't! There are a couple of approaches you can take in your ten minutes.

1. Make a list of all the life admin currently on your plate that needs attending to and then pick a quick one (as making the list could take several minutes).

or

2. Tackle the first task that you think of.

If you have time in your ten minutes to do more than one task, all the better! Of course, if you get into the flow and you don't want to stop – you're liking the hits of the reward chemical dopamine you're getting for ticking things off your list – and you have the time, just keep going.

Alternatively, if you don't manage to complete a task, remember that whatever progress you made in your ten minutes today means you are chipping away at your life admin task pile. And the theory of marginal gains that we looked at in the Introduction means those ten minutes will make a difference; you're closer to ticking a task off your list than if you'd done nothing.

Notice how you feel when your time is up. Did you accomplish more or less than you thought you would in the time you had? Are there any learnings (for example, some tasks aren't as daunting as you thought so putting them off created more anxiety than the task itself) you can take from the experiment that will help you with life admin next time?

TAKEAWAY

Slowly and surely, I'm getting things done.

EXPERIMENT 11

KEEP A GRATITUDE
JOURNAL

Gratitude simply means expressing thanks or appreciation, or feeling grateful for what you have. It's stopping for a moment to recognize the goodness in that moment, in others, in the world – whether it's someone holding the door open for you, the sun shining on your face or a delicious slice of cake.

The key point is the stopping to recognize a moment of goodness and being thankful for it. Absent-mindedly muttering "Thanks" to the person who held open the door you're rushing through isn't really being truly thankful; being aware that holding the door open wasn't an obligatory act, and feeling appreciative that the person chose to do it, is expressing gratitude. That moment of kindness and thoughtfulness in a brief gesture that's over in seconds, can be given a more powerful, and more positive, meaning simply by being aware of it. And that's why we're focusing on a particular way to express this appreciation for this experiment.

Being grateful is not about being polite to other people or beating yourself up because your life isn't as hard as someone else's. Rather, it's simply being aware of what and who in your life is good, what makes you smile, and what you appreciate; and this awareness allows you to feel even more joy in everyday life. It doesn't mean you aren't aware of hardship and difficulties, or that you have less empathy for those who are struggling.

BEING IN THE PRESENT

A drive to try new things and to pursue goals has value, but believing that you'll only be happier when you have, for example, more friends, a new job, or move house, leads to feelings not just of dissatisfaction but even resentment for the life you currently have. Constantly looking ahead to what will make you happy *next* is known as "destination addiction", because you think that success, happiness and a better life is round the next corner[1] – and then the next corner. Taking notice of and being thankful for what's good in your life right now doesn't mean being complacent, but it does help to lessen the need to constantly strive for the next target.

BENEFITS OF BEING GRATEFUL

Scientific studies have tested the effects of gratitude and shown what extraordinary benefits (when practised deliberately) it has. In particular, the research and studies of Robert Emmons, one of the world's leading experts on gratitude,[2] has found that practising gratitude consistently produces significant benefits, such as:

- lower blood pressure
- stronger immune system
- higher levels of positive emotions, such as optimism and happiness
- more generosity and compassion
- less loneliness and isolation.

This may well be because of the following side effects of gratitude.

We take less for granted

Over time, you get used to the new thing you bought, the new place you live in, the new car you drive, and you can take them for granted (this is known as hedonic adaptation[3]). By expressing gratitude, you're appreciating something's value, savouring your enjoyment of it in the moment, as well as eking out more joy or contentment over a longer period of time.

Gratitude counteracts our natural negativity bias

Humans are born with a natural negativity bias, where we focus more on the bad stuff and less on the good stuff.[4] Psychologist Dr Rick Hanson says, "The brain is like Velcro for negative experiences but Teflon for positive ones."[5] By consciously feeling grateful for what's good in your life, you're training your brain to focus on the positives rather than just the negatives.

Gratitude builds resilience

Resilience isn't about not feeling challenges or bad things never happening, and it's not about pushing through difficult feelings or times. Resilience can be strengthened so that you feel better able to cope and actually *are* better able to cope when life throws you a curveball, or seven. Studies show that people who feel and express gratitude can deal with and recover more quickly from serious difficulty or upset.[6]

WHAT IS A GRATITUDE PRACTICE?

A gratitude practice is making time on a regular basis – that's the practice element – to recognize, appreciate and be thankful for what and who is in your life. There are different ways to practise gratitude, and the most common gratitude practice is gratitude journaling – writing down in a notebook what you're grateful for each day.

Robert Emmons and his colleague, Mike McCullough, conducted a controlled experiment where they asked three groups of people to keep a daily diary. One group were asked to write down problems and complications in their life, another group just what happened in their day, and the third group were asked to write down up to five things they were grateful for. The gratitude group showed a considerable rise in happiness and life satisfaction.[7]

HOW TO KEEP A GRATITUDE JOURNAL

- **Write it down**. This is your permission slip for new stationery! You could tap the note into your phone or computer, but the argument for the act of writing down on paper what you're grateful for is that it helps embed it in your memory more effectively.[8] So why not use this as a good reason (or excuse) to start a new notebook? Also, another benefit to writing down your gratitudes is that, when you're having a low moment, you can easily flick back through the pages and see all the good things you've written on previous days. If you feel like you've had a rubbish week, your gratitude journal will be the factual proof that there was good in the past few days.

- **Be detailed**. To get the most from this practice, write down in detail what you appreciate. Being specific about what you're thankful for enables you to appreciate the simple things, the little moments that our days are filled with. For example, rather than saying to yourself that you're grateful for your friend, be more specific: you're grateful that she phoned to see how you are or that he bought you lunch. Gratitudes don't need to be momentous; it's the little things that are the stuff of life that we can find to be thankful for, to hang on to when life is being really challenging. You'll also find more things you're thankful for when you're specific rather than general.

- **Make it easy**. To continue writing in your gratitude journal after this initial experiment, keep your journal in the same spot so you know where to find it – perhaps on your bedside table or next to the coffee mugs in the kitchen. The key with this particular gratitude practice is consistency, so make it easy for yourself by stacking it with another habit (Experiment 31, Make it a Habit).

GET WRITING

For this experiment you can choose to either spend your ten minutes writing down as many things you're grateful for that you can think of, or write down up to five things (as per the study mentioned earlier), even if it takes less than ten minutes.

Remember, you don't need to think of big or "worthy" things to write in your gratitude journal. If you get stuck and struggle to think of anything, focus on the little stuff:

* Your favourite show is back on TV – what is it that you love about the show?
* You got to drink a whole cup of tea before it went cold – how did it feel to have that time?
* Your workmate laughed at your joke – what effect has this had on your interactions?

Your gratitude journal is for you, no one else needs to read it, and as you're the one who will benefit from it, just write whatever you like in it!

TAKEAWAY

There's so much to appreciate in my life.

EXPERIMENT 12

MEDITATE

For this experiment we're going to try meditating. If you're new to the practice, this is a great first step in.

And if you've tried meditation and weren't all that keen, perhaps this is an opportunity to experiment with it once more?

WHAT MEDITATION IS NOT

Let's start with banishing a few myths about meditation.

- It's not emptying your mind or making your mind go blank (give it a go and I'll bet you think of the word "blank").
- You're not trying to banish thoughts or feelings.
- When (not "if", because it will happen) your mind wanders that doesn't mean you're failing or doing it wrong.

- You don't have to sit cross-legged with your eyes closed – you don't even have to be still.
- You don't have to chant (unless you'd like to).
- You don't have to meditate for a long time to benefit, not even for ten minutes!

SO WHAT ACTUALLY IS MEDITATION?

Put very simply, when you meditate you put all your attention on to a point of focus. By doing so, you learn to observe your thoughts and feelings without judging them or being wrapped up in them.

Imagine you're sitting in a garden or park reading a book on a sunny day. You look up and notice the clouds and watch them float across the sky. You aren't in among the clouds, and you aren't thinking about what it feels like to be *in* the clouds; you're not pretending the clouds aren't there, or willing them to travel across the sky more quickly. You simply observe the clouds and then return your attention to the book you're reading.

This is how you learn to treat your thoughts in meditation. When your mind wanders, which it will do, you notice the thoughts and let them drift off – like clouds – then return your attention to the focus of the meditation. Your mind wandering off isn't a sign you're doing anything wrong; it's an opportunity for you to put into practice observing your thoughts, letting them go and returning to the meditation focus.

As you practise, you'll become more aware of your thoughts without engaging with them. Meditation is helpful if you find yourself getting lost in thoughts, raking over the past, replaying conversations, imagining what could go wrong, ruminating... because, with practice, you train yourself to spend less time lost in your worrisome thoughts, which will reduce how stressed you feel.

It's a practice

The benefits of meditation come with practice, with repetition. However, that doesn't mean that if you don't commit to meditating every day, forever more, there's no point in reading on! We're experimenting, remember, so take the pressure off.

This book is about experimenting for ten minutes a day, but if that feels like too long you can reduce it to a couple of minutes – yes really, just two! You will gain more from two minutes' meditation a day than ten minutes once in a blue moon (remember marginal gains?).

The more you practise, the more familiar you'll become with the sensations, with noticing your thoughts and feelings, with letting them go and returning to your point of focus.

HOW YOU BENEFIT FROM MEDITATION

So what will you gain by meditating? Meditation has been around for thousands of years, there are written references dating back to 1500BCE in India, and images dating as far back as 5000BCE.[1] Clearly there's something to it for it to have such longevity.

Unsurprisingly, Western scientists have been very keen to study meditation to find out what that "something" is – what's happening in the brain while meditating.

- Researchers at Stanford University found that meditating reduces your stress levels by lowering your heart rate and your blood pressure.[2]
- A form of meditation known as Mindfulness Based Stress Reduction was developed by US professor Jon Kabat-Zinn and studied by researchers at the University of Massachusetts Medical School. The research study

looked at a group of people with clinical levels of anxiety who practised mindfulness meditation, and discovered that 90% of them experienced a significant reduction in anxiety.[3]

- There are also studies that show meditating regularly can improve the quality of your sleep,[4] as well as your concentration and working memory![5]

GO GENTLY

When you have a busy life, when your mind is occupied from the moment you wake until the moment you go to sleep, doing very little, focusing on just one thing can feel quite strange. When you meditate, your world gets quieter, which means you can become aware of thoughts or feelings that you don't usually (or might not want to) notice.

If you feel fidgety, if you feel uncomfortable with the quiet, it is because you are noticing lots of thoughts pinging into your head or sensations in your body. Go gently.

This is normal, it's not a sign that you can't meditate or there's something wrong, it's just that your world has quietened down so you're noticing what you may not have been aware of before. Acknowledge this is new and unusual, acknowledge whatever you're thinking or feeling, and gently move your attention back to the focus of the meditation. This will probably happen over and over again, and that's okay, it's all part of the process and the experience. So, again, acknowledge your thoughts and/or your bodily sensations and come back to the focus of the meditation.

Guided audio meditations can be helpful in this situation, as they allow you to focus on the voice guiding your meditation.

MAKE MEDITATION SIMPLE

There are myriad ways to meditate – and a similar number of apps available – so you can find a meditation to suit you, how you're feeling, how much time you have or what you want to get out of it.

There are meditations to help you sleep, to bolster your confidence, to build self-compassion, and meditations to move your body to. You can listen to music or gong sounds, keep a tally of how many days you meditate, and even meditate with people on the other side of the world!

Try this now

But let's make it simple to experiment with meditating right now (as long as you're not driving or operating machinery – perhaps put down the kettle too!). You can set a timer for ten minutes or, if you want to take the pressure right off, start the stopwatch on your phone and begin, you'll see at the end how much time has passed.

- Sit, stand or lie down. Close your eyes if you'd like to (not if you're standing), or lower your gaze to a point on the ground to focus on. This reduces the likelihood of you getting distracted by something you can see. Wherever you are, just notice what sounds you can hear. You don't need to have an opinion on the sounds, just notice them.
- Now pay attention to what parts of your body are in contact with whatever you're standing, sitting or lying on. For example, you may notice the soles of your feet pressing on the ground, perhaps your weight is more on one foot than the other. If you're in a chair, you might notice the backs of your thighs pressing against the seat or your elbow resting on the chair arm.
- Any time your thoughts wander off, and they will, that's okay. When you've noticed you've become distracted, gently bring your attention back to your body.

- If you're lying down, notice which parts of your body are in contact with the bed or couch or floor, maybe your head is to one side so one ear is pressed against a pillow. Simply observe, you don't need to judge or change anything.
- Now move your attention to your breath. Do not change anything about how you breathe, just notice the air flow in and out of you. Perhaps it's most noticeable in your chest rising and falling, your stomach expanding and contracting, or maybe you're aware of the air entering and leaving your nose. Follow the natural rhythm of your breath as it flows in and out, without changing anything, without any opinion on how you're breathing.
- Again, when you notice your mind has wandered, gently bring it back to your breath.
- Stay with the observation of your breath for as long as you like.
- Whenever you're ready, move your attention back to your surroundings. Notice your body, any sounds you can hear, be aware of the space you're in.

That's it, your meditation is complete! Have a stretch, a big yawn, a drink of water perhaps, and check your timer to see how long you meditated for.

HOW DOES THIS HELP IN REAL LIFE?

Meditation may seem abstract and separate to real life because you stopped to meditate and now you're getting back on with your day. However, this may be the only time in your day when you experience significant calm. Noticing your mind wandering into other thoughts in meditation teaches you to notice when, in everyday life, you get lost in thought. And it's by noticing you're getting stuck in your head, ruminating or fretting, that you're able to take action to do something about it to calm yourself and bring down your stress levels.

For example, if you walk to work lost in worries about an upcoming meeting you'll arrive feeling frazzled. By learning to notice your thoughts through meditation you're more likely to notice you're worrying about the meeting – and then you can choose whether you want to continue ruminating (and stay in the stress) or switch your attention to the scenery you're walking through (giving yourself the chance to destress).

Ideas for your experiment

- Make a note of how you feel just before and just after meditating – what's the difference?

- Commit to meditating for several consecutive days, and take the same measurements – what do you observe?
- Experiment with meditating at different times of the day in a variety of locations, for shorter or longer periods of time – and collect your data.
- Try one of these apps to help establish a meditation habit: Headspace, Calm, Insight Timer, Buddhify, Unplug.

TAKEAWAY

I notice my thoughts; I am not my thoughts.

EXPERIMENT 13

SAY "NO"
(WITHOUT
FEELING GUILTY)

This is a tricky but oh so rewarding experiment. The act of saying "No" may only take seconds, but when you're someone who struggles to turn anyone down, to decline any request, to set clear boundaries, it can take a lot of thinking time and courage to actually do it. (We dive deeper into boundaries in Experiment 4, Create a Personal Boundary.)

Use your ten minutes today to think about what you want to say no to and how you're going to go about it; then put it into action during the day.

Let's be clear from the start: saying "Yes" is *not* a bad thing. It can feel good to say yes, to be amenable, helpful and make other people happy as well as yourself. But when saying yes is about making other people happy at the *expense of yourself*, of your own joy and peace of mind, that isn't helpful to you.

Rather than bring us closer to the person we're saying a reluctant yes to, which is often why we think we should do it, it disconnects us. By saying yes to something we really want to say no to, we can feel resentful, angry even, that we're having to do a thing we don't want to.

SAYING "NO" CAN BE CHALLENGING

If, for a long time, you've found it hard to say no and you're used to saying yes, and the people around you are used to you saying yes too, it can feel pretty challenging to start using the "no" word. But, remember, it doesn't mean you're never saying yes again, or that you're saying no with zero consideration of the other person.

When someone makes a request of you, it's just that – a request. Do not assume a question is a demand, when in fact the person may just be asking a question. And don't feel you have to give an answer instantly. Even if you feel under pressure (in fact, especially if you feel under pressure), you can give yourself some time by saying you'll get back to the person who's asking. This avoids you giving an automatic "yes" that you might regret, but you're not saying a scary "no" yet either. This also helps the other person understand the answer could go either way, and to not assume it's a "yes". Then, when you're ready to give an answer, you can say no if you want to. Saying yes and then trying to back out later is stressful for you and confusing for the other person.

You might feel a pressure or an expectation to give explanations and excuses for why you're saying no. You might think you're being helpful by explaining, but instead it can come across as being unsure of your "no". If you don't believe in your "no", why would the other person think you mean it?

The other person may take your explanation as an invitation to help you turn your "no" into a "yes". They might try and find reasons for why you don't need to say no and how you can say yes instead. Which means your intention of letting them down gently with an explanation for your no backfires, as the other person thinks it's up for discussion – when it really is not!

Less is more

When saying "no", less is more. Keep it short, simple and say it with a smile.

With an invite, try saying something like, "Thanks for the invite, but I won't be able to come. Have a great time." This response is clear, friendly and signals that this is your complete answer, no discussion required.

With a request for your help, a line like, "I'm sorry, I can't pitch in this time", softens the "no" because you're not saying you'll never help them again, you're leaving the door open to providing future support without committing yourself.

SORRY NOT SORRY

A note on the word "sorry". If it helps you to say "no", feel free to add in "sorry". However, making your decision to decline a request is not something you need to apologize for. What you say yes or no to is your choice, and you don't have to apologize for making your own choices.

Policies and boundaries

Another useful tool when saying no is to make it into a "policy". With a policy, it makes it less personal because you're saying no to the practice rather than the individual. For example, you could say, "It's my policy to take a complete break from work while I eat my lunch", or "I make it a rule that weekends are for family".

In Experiment 4, Create a Personal Boundary we explore the big topic of boundaries and experiment with setting your own.

Consider the flipside

Consider what saying yes (when you don't want to) means you're saying no to – what are the consequences of that "yes"?

For example, if you say yes to taking on more work when you're up against a deadline, you may be saying no to making it home in time for dinner with the family. If you say yes to someone's request to pop round for a coffee, that could mean you're saying no to drinking a cuppa alone with your book, which is what you feel you really need.

TOP TIPS FOR ADDING MORE "NO" INTO YOUR VOCABULARY

- You don't have to start experimenting with saying no by going straight in with flat nos. Begin with saying no to smaller requests that don't feel too scary.
- Buy yourself time to figure out your response by saying you'll come back to them.
- Invoke a "policy", so you're saying no to the practice not the person.
- Remember, you don't need to explain yourself – no is a complete sentence. You are allowed to decline an invitation, a request or even a demand – this does *not* automatically make you a selfish person.

Get comfortable with being uncomfortable

When you've learned, perhaps through your upbringing or society, that saying yes is the helpful, selfless, nice thing to do, it's hard to start saying no instead. It can feel really uncomfortable, rude even, to say no. But you don't feel like that because saying no is the wrong thing to do – it's because it's unusual for you and you're not used to saying no. The good news is that the more you do it, the easier it gets.

So, now you're equipped with the tools to say no to something you don't want to do, time to put it into action!

TAKEAWAY

"No" is a complete sentence.

TEN WAYS TO SAY "NO"

1. No, thank you for asking.

2. Not this time; I'll let you know if anything changes.

3. No, I won't be joining you; hope it goes well.

4. No, I can't help you with that; sorry.

5. That's kind of you to say, but not this time.

6. It's my policy to not...

7. I'm going to pass on this.

8. I have a lot on, so I'm subtracting not adding at the moment.

9. I appreciate you asking, but it's not for me.

10. I'm at capacity right now, so it's a "No".

EXPERIMENT 14

TAKE A MINDFUL WALK

For this experiment we're going outside! We're going to spend our ten minutes being mindful while walking.

You can choose to go for a walk specifically for this experiment, or you can incorporate it into a daily walk you already do: to the station, shops, school pick-up or work. If at all possible, for the first time you try this, walk alone (that means without the dog too), so that you can fully focus for ten minutes on being mindful.

You don't have to be anywhere special to make a walk mindful. It doesn't matter if you're in the heart of a crowded city, on a quiet suburban street or in the depths of the countryside – you can make any walk a mindful one.

Read this chapter, and then decide when you want to put the experiment into action.

MAKE IT MINDFUL

What makes a walk mindful is *where you choose to focus your attention* while you're walking. Sometimes taking a walk is useful for thinking over an issue or for making plans for later. But there are other times when you get stuck in rumination, going over and over the same thoughts without getting anywhere – and that isn't helpful. It's at times like these when applying mindfulness to your walk is beneficial because it brings you out of your thoughts and into the present moment.

In a mindful walk you pay attention to what's going on immediately around you: what you can see, hear, smell and touch right there and then. It pulls your focus out of your head and into the reality of your experience right now. You stop ruminating on a conversation you had or an email you received or a meeting in the future or any of the things on your To Do list. You are simply in the present, experiencing this moment just as it is now.

Being mindful as you walk opens your eyes to the interesting, beautiful, quirky world we live in – whether you're surrounded by nature or on a busy road with noise and bustle all around you. There's a fascinating world out there and we can miss so much if we're too busy lost in thought to look around us. As Ferris Bueller says in the classic eighties movie *Ferris Bueller's Day Off*, "Life moves pretty fast. If you don't stop and look around once in a while, you could miss it." And who are we to argue with Ferris?

The positive consequences of this mindfulness are that as well as interrupting your rumination, studies suggest that mindful walking can reduce depression, anxiety and stress[1] as well as improve how satisfied you are with your life.[2]

What do you need?

Just you! You don't need to walk at a particular speed or have anything with you. Wear what you like, walk where you like – it's not the surroundings that make a walk mindful, it's you.

HOW TO TAKE A MINDFUL WALK

1. Begin by noticing how your body feels.

   o Can you feel the clothes on your skin, how your feet hit the ground with each step, the wind, sun or even rain on your face?
   o Are your shoulders hunched or are your arms swinging loosely by your sides?
   o There's no need to judge what you're noticing or try to change it, simply observe what your body feels like while walking.

2. Now, as you walk, notice what you can see.

   o Perhaps there are trees, bushes, flowers, shops, office
     buildings, people, or vehicles.
   o If it helps to keep you focused, say to yourself, out
     loud or silently in your head, what you can see – the
     colours, shop names, vehicle types, building materials,
     birds.
   o Remember not to judge what you're looking at; there's
     no need to form an opinion, just notice what you can
     see all around you.
   o Move your focus around so that you can take in as
     much of the scene as possible.
   o What can you see when you look down – perhaps
     cracks in the pavement, a flower bed or puddles?
   o What do you notice when you look up – clouds in the
     sky, the roofs of buildings?

3. Next slow down, or even pause, and choose something
   that interests you and focus in on it.

   o For example, a shop window. What's on display? Can
     you recognize what's a product and what's a prop?
     Notice the different sizes, colours and textures you

can see. Is the glass clean or smudged? Is the window frame freshly painted or peeling?

o   Or perhaps you're in a green space – choose a tree or a section of hedge. What colours and shapes are the leaves? Note the spaces between the leaves. Are there other plants mixed in with the hedge? Can you see any insects or signs of birds? What else is living in or growing on the tree?

4. As you resume your walking pace, bring your awareness to your other senses.

o   What you can you hear? Try to single out each individual sound and where it's coming from.

o   Can you detect any particular aromas and their sources?

5. Finish your mindful walk by taking in your environment as a whole:

o   The colours and shapes you can see.

o   The sounds you can hear.

o   The aromas you can smell.

o   The sensations on your skin.

o   How you feel in this place, in this moment in time.

YOUR MIND *WILL* WANDER

While you're taking the mindful walk you will find your mind darts off in different directions and returns to your thoughts. This will happen over and over again, and that's completely normal. It's all part of practising mindfulness – noticing your mind wandering, and then bringing it back to the point of focus; that *is* being mindful.

When you realize your attention has drifted off, don't get annoyed with yourself, you're not doing anything wrong. Simply notice your thoughts wandering and bring your attention back to what you were last focusing on.

If you've completely lost your focus, there are a few ways you can bring your attention to the present moment.

- Check through your senses: note what you can see, hear, smell and feel.
- Say out loud (quietly if you don't want others to hear) what you're noticing with each of your senses, e.g., *red door, car engine, bacon frying, breeze on my face.*
- Focus on your breath: notice where you feel the movement in your chest or stomach as you take a breath in and let it out.

The more you practise this kind of mindful walk, the easier it becomes to notice when your mind has wandered and to bring it back. And the amount of time you're able to focus your attention on the present will lengthen.

IT DOESN'T HAVE TO BE A POST-WORTHY MOMENT

You may want to take photos during your mindful walk. Pausing to photograph something you've noticed as being particularly eye-catching or an interesting detail can help you stay focused on what you're experiencing in that moment.

However, watch out for moving on from taking the photo to editing it, writing a caption, posting it on social media, imagining what other people will think of your photo, waiting for likes and comments... All of this is distracting rather than contributing to your mindful walk; it takes you out of the moment. This mindful walk experiment is only ten minutes long, so wait until the experiment's over before posting your picture.

THE WORLD OPENS UP TO YOU

The beauty of this experiment is that you can try it any time you leave your home. After you've tried a ten-minute mindful walk, you can apply the same process when you quickly nip to the shop or to the post box. If you're enjoying noticing the world around you as you walk, you can keep it going – there's no need to stop at ten minutes if you don't want to!

By looking around you, by paying attention to your environment as you walk through it, you might notice things that you've missed before, from a Victorian post box, intricately detailed iron railings or a cat in a window to an ancient ivy-covered tree, flower buds about to bloom or the sound of a babbling brook.

TAKEAWAY

I am here in this moment.

EXPERIMENT 15

MAKE A MORNING RITUAL

This is an experiment to try before you do anything, and I mean ANYTHING at the start of your day.

It's so easy for the day to run away from you the moment you get up. You see a stack of emails on your phone, the kids want feeding, you've nothing ready to wear, there's an early meeting scheduled… You'd like to fit in a yoga class, time for meditation and journaling (See Experiment 12, Meditate and Experiment 30, Try Freestyle Journaling), perhaps go for a run, or just get up leisurely with a coffee. Carving out a chunk of time for *you* seems impossible, so none of those things on your wish list happens, instead you tear through the morning feeling rushed, stressed and behind from the get-go.

What if there was another way? A path through the middle where you could set yourself up for the day with calm and intention without having to set the alarm hours earlier or abandoning your life to live in a hut on the side of a remote mountain?

Here, we'll look at three different ways to start off your day before you even get out of bed. All three together can be done within ten minutes, or choose just one if you want to be super quick (and experiment with what impact a one-minute action has on you). As this experiment is designed for the start of the day, you may want to read it through now and put it into action tomorrow morning.

1: NAME WHAT YOU'RE THANKFUL FOR

Before your brain goes straight into thinking about how low in energy you are, how little sleep you've had, how you've too much to do in not enough time today – i.e. all the areas you feel you're lacking – take a few moments to focus on what you *do* have. I'm not suggesting you do this in a "I should be grateful and shut up" way – making yourself feel bad about your thoughts doesn't help. You're allowed to feel however you're feeling, and we're not trying to deny your tiredness or invalidate your To Do list. What we're doing with this experiment is *also* giving some space in your brain to what's good in your life.

On waking, perhaps before you even open your eyes, simply name five things you're thankful for. The more specific you can be with these five things, the more meaningful it will be for you (see Experiment 11, Keep a Gratitude Journal).

For example, five things you appreciate could be:

1. the comfortable bed you've just slept in
2. a friend texting last night
3. a favourite song playing on the radio right now
4. your child falling asleep before you finished the story last night
5. yesterday's meeting ending on time.

You may be able to think of five gratitudes quite quickly (in which case feel free to name more!), or it may take you a little longer to name five, but I encourage you to keep going. You can say them silently in your head or out loud, either to yourself or share them with your partner or family.

2: LIST WHAT YOU'RE LOOKING FORWARD TO

Once you've looked back at what you're thankful for, next you're going to look forward to what joys lie ahead. What you're looking forward to doesn't have to be big, like a holiday or an anniversary, it can be small and specific to you.

If you think something is too insignificant or silly to name, but you really are looking forward to it, then list it! It doesn't matter how trivial someone else might find it – this isn't someone else's list, it's yours. If it makes you smile or lifts your heart to think of it, it counts.

Think of five things you're looking forward to and, if at all possible, choose what's happening in the near future – today ideally – rather than in a month's time, because that will help add to your anticipatory joy.

For example, five things you're looking forward to could be:

1. wearing the new coat you bought as a sale bargain
2. a lunchtime walk around the park
3. listening to a new episode of your favourite podcast
4. cuddling your dog
5. your partner making dinner for the family tonight.

Focusing a little attention for a little time on what there is to look forward to in your day, what little (or big) joys, moments of calm or connection you anticipate in the coming hours doesn't mean you're ignoring the difficulties or challenges in your day. It's merely giving you the opportunity to acknowledge the light in your day as well as the dark.

And by starting your day with this broader, more balanced perspective, you're less likely to feel grumpy and on the back foot, and more likely to feel positive and ready to handle whatever comes up. Give it a go and see for yourself.

3: SET AN INTENTIONAL MANTRA

A mantra is a word or phrase that you repeat, often silently in your head to yourself. Depending on the mantra, it can give you a positive or negative message. Without realizing it, you may have been repeating unintentional mantras to yourself for years – words like "tired", "bored" or "Idiot".

Repeating the same words over and over have an impact because they're a message that you're giving yourself over and over. If you keep calling yourself an "idiot", it makes it harder to believe you're capable of working through a challenge, solving a problem, reaching a goal or anything that requires self-belief and confidence.

Again (I'm sure you're getting the gist now I'm not one for toxic positivity, as mentioned in the Introduction), this is not about faking cheeriness, pretending you're not tired or don't have a challenging day ahead. This is about acknowledging the reality of your circumstances and your feelings, *and* how you want to feel and be today as well.

So, first of all, think about how you *want* to feel, how you want to behave as you go through this day. Perhaps you want to feel light or playful or brave. Maybe you want to be strong or focused or patient. You can use the guiding word you chose in Experiment 1, or you may want to use a different word specific to this day. For example, you may have chosen "nurture" for your guiding word for the experimental month. However, today you're facing a tricky meeting at work where you want to feel confident, self-assured and composed, so the word you may want to repeat to yourself as a mantra at the start of *this* day is "calm" or "breathe". Or you might repeat a phrase several times to yourself – for example, "Got this", "Slow and steady" or "Bring it on".

Once you've chosen a word or phrase, repeat your mantra to yourself, out loud or silently, several times over. Let your mantra and its supportive meaning soak into you; picture yourself embodying this word as you go through the day.

As you've carried out this experiment right at the start of your day, you're already winning at life! Make a mental, or actual, note of how you feel following this experiment, then get on with your day.

TAKEAWAY

I choose how I start my day.

EXPERIMENT 16

CHOOSE YOUR
CHEERLEADING SQUAD

For this experiment, you're going to choose your own imaginary squad of cheerleaders – a group of people you would like to bring to mind any time you need support, encouragement, advice or inspiration.

The beauty of an imaginary cheerleading team is that you can have ANYONE you like on your side. They don't need to be flesh-and-blood folk you know in real life. Your teammates can be living or dead, they could be famous celebrities, historical figures, fictional characters, or people you know have got your back, either now or in the past.

What matters is that the people you choose feel supportive, that when you think of them you feel like they're cheering you on. They can be inspiring, wise, funny, irreverent... as long as you feel that, in your imagination, they're backing you all the way.

Fill your cheerleading squad with people that you look to for guidance, to make you laugh, to bring you back down to earth, to reassure or inspire or whatever you're looking for at a tricky moment. Whether you're feeling nervous before giving a speech, stuck on what to cook for dinner or wondering how to start a difficult conversation, there can be someone in your squad who could help you. You can call upon your squad members at any time of day or night, in any circumstances, because they live in your imagination.

HOW TO PICK YOUR SQUAD

There are different approaches you can take when thinking about who you want in your imaginary cheerleading squad. You could simply go for people you like and admire. Or you could be more methodical and list out the areas of your life you feel are most challenging, or any particular issues you're currently facing, and then think about who would be most supportive in these areas. You might choose them because of something you've heard them say, a character they've played, or you find it empowering to imitate their persona or physical presence.

Remember, this team is imaginary so you don't need to get caught up in logistics of how to get in touch with them.

There's no minimum or maximum number of cheerleaders to have in your team. But you do want to be able to remember who's in your squad so you can bring them to mind when needed, so perhaps aim for somewhere between three and six.

Choose who you want in your squad because you really want them, not who you think you *should* have. Joan of Arc or Albert Einstein might be worthy members, but if you don't actually want them in your team, they don't get a place! And if you find yourself getting bogged down with wondering who would want to be in your squad or if they'd get along with other members, remember this is all imaginary – it's a fun way to feel supported, so team politics don't apply here!

Potential team players

Who you want on your team is up to you, not anyone else. Here are a few suggestions for where you could look for your squad members:

- Athletes
- Activists
- Writers
- Artists
- Actors
- Comedians

- Scientists
- Explorers
- Politicians
- Fictional characters
- Significant people from your past, e.g. teachers or grandparents
- Valued people from your present, e.g. family members, friends or colleagues

INSPIRING WORDS

You might like to think of an inspirational quote to go with each member of your squad. Here are a few examples:

- Maya Angelou: "You may encounter many defeats, but you must not be defeated."[1]
- Bob Marley: "Every little thing gonna be alright."[2]
- Dory, *Finding Nemo*: "Just keep swimming."
- Steve Jobs: "Your time is limited, so don't waste it living someone else's life."[3]
- Nadiya Hussain: "I can and I will."[4]

If there's a quote, a song lyric or a line from a poem you especially love and keep coming back to whenever you're feeling challenged, maybe the person responsible for those words or who you associate with them would make a supportive member of your squad?

USING YOUR SQUAD

Once your cheerleading team is formed, they're with you any time you need or want to call on them.

When to use examples

- If you're feeling anxious, bring to mind a calm member of your team and imagine what they would say to you, or perhaps they'd give you a hug.
- If you're frustrated with a difficult problem, which squad member could help you to change perspective or encourage you to keep going? What would they say or do, how would they handle this situation?
- If you're having a confidence wobble, think of who in your team can give your self-belief a boost and picture them standing beside you.

Some members of your team might stay there for years, seeing you through life's good, bad and in-between times. Others might take their place for a particular dilemma or period of your life before vacating their spot for the next person.

Your team sheet

What would help you to bring your cheerleading squad to mind when you need them? Here are a few ideas:

- Keep a list of your squad in the Notes app on your phone.
- Find photos for each team member, print them out and stick them on a wall so you can chat to them whenever you feel like it.
- Share your squad and why you've chosen each member on social media, you could start a discussion or inspire someone else to create their own squad.
- Start a conversation with your friends about this experiment, and ask who they'd have on their team.

Remember: this is an experiment, so if some of your team members don't feel right you can always drop them from your squad and bring in a new signing!

TAKEAWAY

My cheerleading squad have got my back.

EXPERIMENT 17

SCHEDULE "WORRY TIME"

If you're someone prone to worrying, to getting distracted by rehashing what happened in the past or imagining what could go wrong in the future, you'll know how disruptive it is, and what a detrimental effect it has on your wellbeing.

Worrisome thoughts interrupt and pull you away from the present moment. They take the shine off what's going well or right in life because your mind focuses on what could go wrong. Worrying uses up your energy and your head space and, as so often whatever you're worrying about doesn't come to fruition, it can be a waste of your time too.

So, instead of thinking about your worries and fears throughout the day, whenever a distressing thought comes to you, experiment with scheduling Worry Time.

WHAT IS WORRY TIME?

Worry Time is a specific time of your day that you devote to worrying – sounds a bit strange, right? But, as a CBT (cognitive behavioural therapy) technique known as "stimulus control training", it's been found to be highly effective. Instead of feeling like you're at the mercy of your worrisome thoughts at any time of day or night, you are able to take back some control by allocating a particular time – and place – where you're going to give those worries the spotlight.

Scheduling Worry Time has been shown to make a difference to how much worriers worry. A study by researchers at the University of Illinois was carried out with people who spend a significant amount of time each day worrying.[1] The participants were asked to choose a specific time and place where they would spend 30 minutes focusing on their worries. During that specified time, they were to concentrate their attention on their worries, and try to find solutions where applicable. If a spontaneous worry popped into their head at any other time of day, they were to delay thinking about it until the specified time. The results of the study showed that doing this each day for two weeks had a significant reduction on how much they worried. It also improved the participants' quality of sleep.

MAKE IT DOABLE FOR YOU

While the study devoted 30 minutes to Worry Time, we're going to use our ten minutes instead. These experiments are all about boosting your wellbeing in doable ways (you're welcome to spend longer if you choose to!).

How to create Worry Time

1. **Time**. Choose the time of day you're going to allocate as your Worry Time. If possible, pick a time at least three hours before bed so that your worries can't leak into the time when you're wanting to wind down to sleep. A time at the end of your workday or before you start making dinner might work well.

2. **Place**. Decide on a location where you're going to spend your Worry Time, so that you have a specific spot and a concrete plan to deal with your worries.

3. **Worry Time**. At the prescribed time and place, give your worries your full attention for ten minutes. Talk them through out loud or write down what's troubling you to work out counter arguments or possible solutions. This is your time to give what's stressing and upsetting your full focus. It's possible that you may find you don't need the full ten minutes. The act of delaying giving your worries airtime until this specified time can mean some of them lose their potency, and not seem so worrisome anymore.

4. **End**. When your allocated time is up, your window of Worry Time is closed. You have the same time and place scheduled for the next day, so if you're still angsting about your worries, your next Worry Time is just shy of 24 hours away. And of course, as this is an experiment, you can tweak any issues with the process and try again.

WORRYING OUTSIDE OF WORRY TIME

Any time a worrisome thought appears, that isn't urgent and doesn't need to be dealt with straight away, tell yourself you'll deal with it at Worry Time. Then you're free to put your focus and energy on whatever you were in the middle of. If you worry that you'll forget the worry (one could argue if you can forget the worry, is it that big of a worry?), make a quick note of it to look at it later.

Remember to be kind to yourself when worries pop up. Everyone worries sometimes, and berating yourself for it won't make you feel any better. Be self-compassionate, give yourself a break and know that you've got this experiment of Worry Time to help you.

TAKEAWAY

I'll deal with it in Worry Time.

EXPERIMENT 18

STRENGTHEN YOUR CONNECTIONS

Desiring a sense of belonging, to feel connected to our fellow humans, is built into us – we're "hardwired for connection".[1] Back in cave-dwelling days it was vital that we had strong connections to others because our literal survival depended on it. We needed each other to protect ourselves from being eaten by tigers and bears. While we're a lot less likely to find a hungry bear roaming our neighbourhood nowadays, we still have that need and thirst for connection. Which is why today's experiment focuses on strengthening your connections.

WELLBEING BOOST

Several research studies have found that social relationships – ongoing connections with a partner, family, friends, neighbours or your community – have a positive impact on your wellbeing. People who are socially connected live longer than those with few social ties, regardless of their physical health. Scientists have found a few reasons for this:[2]

- Social ties increase healthy behaviour, such as eating well and exercising.
- Social support with people who help you emotionally benefits your mental health.
- Supportive connections positively affect your body's ability to deal with stress and immunity.

Of course, unhealthy relationships work in the opposite way. If you only spend time with people who engage in self-destructive behaviour, you're in an unhappy marriage or your relationships are toxic, that's going to have a decidedly negative impact on your wellbeing.

When you stop to think about it, you know the people in your life who have a positive effect on your wellbeing. There will be people (could be one person or several) with whom you feel a real connection. Spending time with them feels good, they may challenge you but they don't drain you.

This is not about how many people you're friends with, how long you've known them, whether you see them in person or only online, or even about being related to them. The social relationships that are beneficial for your mind and body – and, perhaps, your soul – are those that simply feel good to you, whatever they look like. And these connections are worth spending a little time cultivating and strengthening.

NOURISH YOUR RELATIONSHIPS

Healthy relationships require attention, a little TLC (tender, loving care), to be mutually beneficial. There are different ways you can strengthen your connections depending on the person/ people and your circumstances. Choose from these ideas (or come up with your own) to spend ten minutes on nourishing one or more of your relationships:

- **Book a date**. Even if you've been together for decades (perhaps especially if you've been together for decades) arrange a chunk of time for just the two of you to do something that's out of your ordinary routine.
- **Phone a friend**. Just to chat, catch up, see how they are and to connect.
- **Show your gratitude**. Do something unexpected to demonstrate your appreciation (see Experiment 7, Perform Random Acts of Kindness).

- **Go tech-free**. Put away your phone when talking face-to-face; research shows that just having a phone in sight (you don't even have to be using it) interferes with how close and connected the people in conversation feel.[3]
- **Listen**. Actively listen to the other person, making eye contact as they speak, picking up on their body language as well as their words, reflecting back what they've said to make sure you understand them and asking open-ended questions. Empathize, listen without judgement and allow moments of silence in case there's more they want to say, rather than jumping in with unsolicited advice or comparing their life or struggle with your own. This will help them to feel really heard and deepen your connection with them.
- **Celebrate**. What good things are going on in your friends' and loved ones' lives? Be their cheerleader by congratulating, praising and making a fuss of them.
- **Hug**. If you're the hugging kind (not everyone is), physical contact is a great way to boost levels of oxytocin – known as "the cuddle hormone" – which increases bonding, building trust and compassion.[4]

TAKEAWAY

I nourish and nurture my valued relationships.

EXPERIMENT 19

SAVOUR AND DELIGHT

This experiment is all but guaranteed to make you feel great! It's all about "savouring". Savouring is not only about enjoying what feels good, but being *aware* of that joy.

Researchers describe savouring as "generating, intensifying and prolonging enjoyment".[1] Savouring is different to pleasure because of the mindfulness factor required – to "savour" requires you to have awareness of what is pleasurable.

DIFFERENT SAVOUR FLAVOURS

There are three kinds of savouring:

1. **Present**. By being in the present moment you mindfully relish what's delightful in the here and now. For example, when you take the first sip of an ice-cold drink on a baking hot day and you revel in its deliciousness.

2. **Past**. You recall and reminisce about happy moments and experiences from your past – for example, when you have a flashback to a moment your friend had you in fits of giggles.
3. **Future**. By imagining what's going to happen, you anticipate the delightful experience to come. For example, as you traipse home in the rain from a long day at work, you fantasize about how wonderful it will be to snuggle up with your cat in front of a roaring fire.

While you may have lots going on in your life, with your attention being pulled in many directions, there are opportunities to savour throughout your day.

SAVOURING BOOSTS YOUR WELLBEING

Not only does the moment when you're savouring feel good in itself, savouring is also hugely beneficial. Studies have found that savouring can *increase* optimism, life satisfaction and happiness, and *decrease* stress, guilt and depression.[1] Plus, those who savour more often are more able to remain cheerful even when their day isn't packed with delightful events.[2]

Interestingly, in this instance money does NOT help; a study found that wealthier people are less able to savour and therefore miss out on its benefits.[3]

WAYS TO SAVOUR

Now you know how great for your wellbeing savouring is, how can you go about it?

- **Find your happy place**. Think of a particular place that holds a happy memory for you. Somewhere that just thinking of it makes you smile. Close your eyes and bring to mind that location; picture the scene in detail: what you could hear, smell and touch, any other people who were there. Immerse yourself in the warm glow of that memory, inhabit the joy you felt.
- **Reminisce with others**. Remind friends or family of an experience you shared that thrilled you, made you all laugh, gave you a sense of awe or amazement. Retell the story together, remembering the quirky moments that make it a cherished memory.
- **Pay attention** Being mindful allows you to notice when there is something worth savouring because you spend more time in the present moment. So, when you notice that something is delighting you, whether it's a child's hug, a TV show making you laugh or completing a puzzle, pause for a moment to relish and revel in that moment.
- **Tune into your senses**. Maximize your enjoyment of a sensation by focusing on it. Shut out distractions (TV, phone, book, other people) to concentrate on listening to

a favourite song, eating a juicy apple or brushing your hair, and luxuriate in the sensation.

- **Picture it**. Find a photo (in an album, on your phone or in a frame on display) that captures a joyful moment in your life and study it, recalling when and where the photo was taken. Think back to what was happening, how you were feeling, who was there – in front and behind the photo – and savour the memory.

For this experiment, give over your ten minutes to revelling in delight and joy. Choose one idea from the list above (or choose your own idea) and devote 1% of your time today to savour the memory, experience the sensation. Notice how you feel before and after to see what difference taking time to savour makes to you.

TAKEAWAY

Savouring is the flavouring of life.

EXPERIMENT 20

UNCOVER YOUR INNER STRENGTH

After going through a difficult period in our lives – maybe experiencing sudden change, upset or grief – we might want to forget it ever happened. If it was a time of pain and struggle, it's understandable that we want to get away from those feelings and memories.

However, by pushing it aside we could be missing out on a powerful source of information that will benefit us the next time we're faced with adversity (let's face it, challenges will keep showing up, as that's life as a human). In the space of even a short period of time (like the ten minutes you have right now), recalling past difficulties can uncover strengths along with coping strategies for the future. Specifically, *writing* about your past difficulties has been found to be beneficial: it can strengthen resilience as well as decrease rumination and how stressed you feel.[1]

In this experiment, you're going to take ten minutes to write about a challenging time in your past.

SELECTING AN EXPERIENCE FROM YOUR PAST

Just to be clear: this is *not* about ripping open old wounds or retraumatizing yourself. The aim here is not to recall a highly upsetting and painful experience, but to revisit a difficult time in your past from which you've gained some emotional distance and can observe with a little more perspective.

You are free to choose the challenging experience you want to write about – there's no criteria for it to meet, no minimum level of difficulty for it to hit. You may be more comfortable with recalling an older rather than recent experience but, truly, it's entirely up to you.

The short period of time you're writing for (ten minutes) gives you the opportunity to focus your mind without drawing you in too deep into past pain. The writing prompts below will guide you through unearthing the rich wisdom lying within your experience that can support and benefit you in future challenges.

TAKE CARE

A few points to bear in mind before you begin:

- Be intentional about your reason for entering into this experiment – it is to gain perspective on the past, explore what helped you at the time and what you can take from the experiment to support you in the future. The experiment is not an excuse to ruminate or berate yourself for perceived failures.

- Although you're only spending ten minutes on this writing exercise, creating a quiet, relaxed space for yourself where you won't be disturbed and where you feel comfortable will help you feel supported as you work through it.

- To complete this experiment and move on from it when you've finished writing, you may find it helpful to move yourself physically. Try getting up from where you've been writing, shaking out your arms and legs, taking a few deep breaths in and sighing your breath out, and move on to something completely different.

- If you find that the experience you recalled has stirred up more upset than you anticipated, please do seek support from a medical professional – take care of yourself.

- And remember, as with all the experiments, it's your choice whether or not you want to explore this one.

WRITING PROMPTS

You're welcome to write as freely and expressively as you like about the challenging time in your past. To help guide you through the experiment so that you can explore how you weathered the storm and emerged from it, here are some writing prompts you may like to use:

- What helped you to navigate that time in your life? (For example, going for daily walks, drinking less alcohol, going to bed early, dropping things from your To Do list.)
- Who gave you support? (For example, offloading to a good friend, your boss lightening your workload, another parent doing the school pick-up, neighbours cooking dinner for you.)
- What have you learned about yourself from that time that you're proud of? (For example, you're stronger than you thought, you can cope with sudden change, you're resourceful.)
- What can you take from that experience to help you with future challenges? (For example, it's okay to ask for help, time alone is important, spending time in nature helps.)

WRITE TO YOURSELF

An alternative for this experiment is to write a letter from your present self to your past self. With the passage of time, further life experience and perspective what would you like to tell a past you, the you who's in the thick of that adversity? What does past you need to hear? What words of support, encouragement and love can you give to them?

Yet another option is to write a letter to your future self from your present self with a message for when you're experiencing a difficult time in the future. Keep the letter somewhere safe so that you in the future can read your own words of advice and reassurance. This letter could serve to remind you of your resilience and strength, of the value in asking for help and from whom, and of what practical actions you can take to support yourself.

So, if you would like to, take ten minutes to bring to light your coping strategies, your resilience and your strength by experimenting with writing about a difficult experience, and what you can take from that experience to help you in the future.

TAKEAWAY

There is wisdom in my past.

EXPERIMENT 21

HAVE FUN AND PLAY

As the title suggests, this experiment is about having fun – letting go of anything serious and allowing yourself to kick back, play and just mess about!

Simple, right? Well, perhaps not. Sometimes it can be quite tricky to think about how to enjoy yourself, to identify what would be a fun thing to do and to allow yourself to play. Because playing is for children, isn't it?

Stuart Brown, psychiatrist and author of *Play. How it shapes the brain, opens the imagination and invigorates the soul*, disagrees. Brown argues, "We are designed to be lifelong players, built to benefit from play at any age".[1]

To "play" is to do something for the joy of it. It isn't a means to an end – for a bigger plan or a deadline or to have something to show at the end of it. And play is not something to be judged by others. There is no purpose to play, other than the fun derived from doing it.

Rather than waiting to have fun when we have the time for it, Brown says that it is more beneficial to "infuse life with play" so it features in your everyday, rather than happening on occasion.

A WORD ON CREATIVITY

Creativity is part of play, but that word can be a sticking point if you think that to be creative you have to be able to draw or knit or write poetry or create a thing to a certain standard. *Everyone* is creative.

YES, EVERYONE IS CREATIVE, INCLUDING YOU!

You express your creativity every day, you just might not recognize it. Your creativity is in the clothes you choose to wear, the stories you make up for your nephew, the photographs you take (including the pictures on your phone), the presentation you make at work, the meals you cook.

Creativity is not the sole preserve of those with the label "artist"; no one gets to rule on who is and is not allowed that title.

PLAY FOR GROWN-UPS

If you're finding it difficult to think what play really looks like to you, take a trip down memory lane. Remember what you loved to do as a child. What did you most enjoy doing? What grabbed and kept your attention? If it made you happy when you were a child, there's a good chance you'll enjoy the same or a similar activity as an adult.

Here are a few examples of play:

- **Reading**. Picking up a book for pleasure, not because it's a set text or papers for work.
- **Travelling**. Exploring a different part of your city or another country.
- **Listening to music**. Experiencing music moves you – feeling your physical or mental reaction to it.
- **Creating**. Making art, writing, baking, sewing, gardening...
- **Playing an instrument or singing**. Making music and song for pure enjoyment; not working toward a performance.
- **Watching a movie**. Choosing a movie that entertains, enthrals and fascinates you.
- **Going to the theatre**. Experiencing a live performance, be it a play, a musical, a dance performance, a band or a comedy set.

- **Learning**. Choosing a new language, a new recipe, an instrument for the enjoyment and without judgement.
- **Playing sport**. The word "play" is built right in to this experience!

How you play – what you find fun, enjoyable, energizing, relaxing or nourishing – depends entirely on you; you alone get to decide what play and fun means for you.

PERFECTIONISM

Something that can get in the way of embracing play is pesky old perfectionism. Perfectionism is often mistakenly limited to the desire to want things to be perfect – but it's more than that. Behind perfectionism are fears of:

- making a mistake
- looking foolish
- not doing or being good enough
- being judged or criticized.

While you might recognize this in more serious settings, such as the workplace, it can creep into all areas of life, even encroaching on something that's supposed to be fun. Because the fear isn't only of other people seeing we got something wrong, looked silly, weren't good enough and criticizing us for it, it's also because we can be the (sometimes the worst) judge of ourselves. We don't want to let ourselves down, to not meet our own expectations, to do something badly, to feel inadequate or foolish. (See the Introduction for how experimenting helps me with my own perfectionist tendencies.)

Perfectionists often think they can keep themselves safe by *not trying*. In the process, when it comes to play at least, they miss out on the potential for enormous fun and enjoyment.

If you need any more encouragement to play, research has found that playful adults are more active, more satisfied with their lives,[2] feel less stressed and employ healthier coping strategies when facing challenges.[3] So, through play not only do you get to simply enjoy yourself, it can be very beneficial for your wellbeing!

LET'S PLAY

Time to flex your playful muscles in this experiment. If play feels daunting to you, remember you're only messing about for ten minutes and there's no "right" way to play.

Take a look at these suggestions for how you can play, or come up with your own:

- **Create a playlist**. Gather together your favourite upbeat tunes, and sing and dance along to them as energetically as you like.
- **Solve puzzles**. Have a go at a wordsearch, crossword, sudoku, or a brain teaser.
- **Write a poem**. Remember poetry doesn't always have to rhyme; try your hand at a limerick, haiku or sonnet.
- **Get messy**. Whether you're painting a wall, planting vegetables or baking with children, don't worry about the mess you're making of yourself or the space you're in. Savour the feeling of paint on your skin, dirt under your nails and flour on your face right at this moment. You can clean up when you've finished.
- **Play games**. There is an abundance of ways to play games these days: on the computer, phone or games console; or go old school with a deck of cards or hopscotch. When out and about try eye-spy or traffic snooker (spot cars in the correct colour order). At home, play along with a quiz on the TV or radio.
- **Find fun in nature**. Make a daisy chain, whistle with a blade of grass, whittle a stick, find animals in clouds or roll down a hill.
- **Make up stories**. Fire up your imagination by coming up with a new bedtime story for your children, or create a tale in your head about your fellow commuters.

- **Build**. Treat yourself to a Lego kit or an AirFix model.
- **Experiment with arts and crafts**. Try photography, papercutting, knitting, crocheting, printing, writing, drawing, painting, sewing, etc.
- **Learn a new language**. Choose a foreign language and learn "hello", "goodbye", "please" and "thank you" or a couple of fun phrases. (Side note: when I was a child I learned how to ask, "Where is the toilet?" in six different languages. Sadly, I could rarely understand the answer.)
- **Read**. Pick up a novel, biography or a magazine and read for ten minutes for your own pleasure.
- **Make music**. Sing, hum, tap out a rhythm with your hands on a surface or play an instrument.
- **Colour in** Treat yourself to an adult (or children's) colouring in, dot-to-dot or sticker book.
- **Watch and laugh**. Hunt out video clips of your favourite stand-up comedian or comedy show for an injection of laughter.

So, how are you going to experiment with playing, mucking about and having fun for ten minutes?

TAKEAWAY

I'm never too busy (or too old) to have fun.

EXPERIMENT 22

MAKE A LIFE WHEEL

If your life is feeling out of kilter, and you'd like to find more balance, a useful tool is an exercise known as a life wheel. The concept of a life wheel, or wheel of life, was first created by Paul I Meyer, founder of the US-based Success Motivation Institute®. The idea is that you take a snapshot of your life now and look at the different areas of your life: what feels good, what is getting your attention, what feels lacking, and what in your life needs more of your time and care.

The life wheel helps you to see which areas of your life are currently fulfilling you – giving you satisfaction and joy – and which areas are not meeting your needs – leaving you dissatisfied or frustrated. Using the image of a wheel is one way to divide your life into sections, but if you wanted to you could use cups or buckets to represent each area of your life instead.

You can take ten minutes to go through this exercise today, and then once a month, follow up with a check-in to see how your life is feeling and where you may want to give some attention for the next few weeks.

CREATE YOUR LIFE WHEEL

Step 1

List out the key areas of your life, for example:

- Partner
- Family
- Friends
- Career/work
- Health
- Pleasure
- Education
- Community
- Finances
- Spirituality

You don't have to include all these items; your list may look different to someone else's and that's okay. It's the areas that you feel are most important in your life that you want on your wheel. Use whatever words or labels you feel most appropriate for you. You'll probably end up with around five to nine different areas.

Step 2

On a piece of paper, draw a small circle, then draw another circle round the first one, then three more circles so that you now have five circles within each other, evenly spaced apart. This is your wheel. Draw lines (or spokes) from the centre of the wheel to the outer edge to create as many segments as match the defined areas of your life. On the outer edge of the wheel, label each segment with the areas from your list. See the example below.

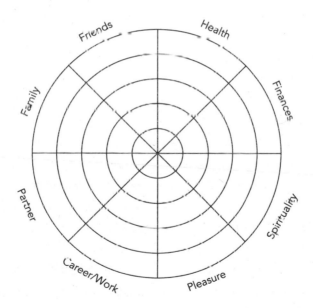

Step 3

The centre point of your wheel represents a score of zero, each of the inner rings denotes two points, which takes you up to a score of ten at the outer edge of your wheel. If it helps you can write zero in the centre and ten at the outer edge of each segment of your wheel.

Taking each segment in turn, consider how you feel about that area of your life. For example, how you feel about your relationships with your friends – how much time you spend together, how you communicate; or how you feel about your health – what you do to look after your wellbeing.

GUT REACTIONS

The benefit of only taking ten minutes to do this is that you don't have time to overthink it. Go with your gut reaction and give each area of your life a score out of ten. Remembering that a score of zero is at the centre of the wheel and ten at the outer edge, shade in with a pencil or coloured pens each section from the centre of the wheel up to where you've marked. For example, if you scored Health 5/10, you'll shade in halfway up the Health segment. Or if you scored Work 8/10, you'll shade in all but the final ring of the Work segment.

When you've scored each area of your life and shaded in each segment up to that score, you'll end up with something like this:

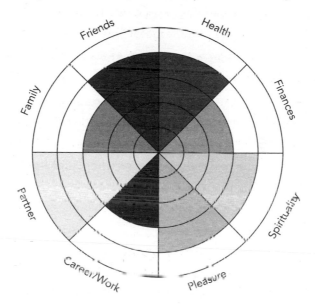

USING YOUR LIFE WHEEL

Your completed life wheel clearly shows how you feel about the different areas of your life. There's a good chance you haven't fully shaded in all of the segments. You might find some sections are barely filled in compared to others. That's okay, you are where you are. This exercise isn't about getting you to have your entire wheel completely filled in – expecting every part of your life to have all your attention, to feel your absolute best at all times, is a big ask!

Consider the possible reasons behind how you've scored your life wheel. Perhaps your Family segment is mostly filled up because you've just been on holiday together with no other distractions. Or maybe your Pleasure section has only been shaded in up to the 2-point mark because you've been so busy with a work project you haven't had time for hobbies or fun.

Set some goals

Take one segment of your life wheel at a time and think about what score you'd like it to have. With your responsibilities, demands on your time, your current energy you may not be looking for 10/10 everywhere, perhaps you'd feel good about reaching 7 or 8. Mark that goal on your segments with a thick pen or pencil line.

Decide on your action

Now you've got your life wheel, you know which areas of your life you want to give some attention to, and you can decide what action you're going to take to increase the score in that segment of your wheel.

To begin with, choose one action for one segment that will take you one step closer to where you want to be on your wheel (remember, we're all about making this doable!).

Here are a few action examples to get you thinking:

- **Partner**. Organize a date night.
- **Friends**. Invite your friend over for coffee.
- **Career**. Update your CV.
- **Community**. Check in on your neighbour.
- **Education**. Download an app to help you learn a new language.
- **Health**. Book a dental appointment.
- **Family**. Play a board game.
- **Finances**. Make a list of income and expenditure for the month to compare with next month.
- **Spirituality**. Spend ten minutes meditating.
- **Pleasure**. Read a chapter of your current bedside book.

This is where the theory of micro-gains (flip back to the Introduction for a reminder) comes into play again. You don't have to make massive changes to increase all the areas of your life wheel: choose one section, decide on one step you can take, and then – here's the crucial bit – take action.

TAKEAWAY

My life wheel is evolving (and revolving!).

EXPERIMENT 23

DESIGN A CALM CORNER

To be clear, this experiment is not about making your house look Pinterest-worthy or trying to compete with show homes on Instagram. This is about creating a little nook, a small sanctuary space, in your home where you can retreat to for a few (or many) moments of calm and peace. If you have an entire room going spare, all power to you, but let's work on the basis your home isn't a mansion; in many homes these days, most rooms are multi-tasking (home office in the corner of your living room, working from your kitchen table?) and space to claim for yourself can be limited.

WHAT IS A CALM CORNER?

A calm corner is a little area of your home – it doesn't need to take up any more space than a corner of your bedroom, if that's what's available to you – that you can claim as yours; it is a place you can go for some downtime, some respite from the busyness of life.

The point of dedicating a specific spot in your home as a calm corner is that it marks it out for that purpose. Consequently, you will associate that nook with peace, with taking a breather, with time for yourself. Every time you sit in that special place you know this is a moment for *you*. It's the more realistic, practical and cheaper version of going to a spa hotel every time you're in need of a break.

You may find that sitting in your chair with a cuppa and journal first thing in the morning gets your day off to a calm start. Or perhaps sitting in your sanctuary spot when you get home from work helps you decompress from the day. It may be that a few minutes in your cozy nook helps you cope with the kids' chaotic bedtime. It may even be the place you dedicate to reading your daily experiment from this book!

CHOOSING YOUR CORNER

Where you create your calm corner depends on the space available in your home. Enough room for a chair would be great, but a couple of cushions or pillows on the floor will work too. If possible, choose a room for your calm corner that isn't used by the whole household all the time (which is why your bedroom is often ideal).

The rest of the room doesn't need to be a Zen palace (although that would be lovely, obviously), so don't stress out about tidying up/fixing the rickety chest of drawers/redecorating or let those things stop you from cracking on with creating your calm corner. Making and keeping one little nook nice is a lot more achievable than reconfiguring a whole room (you're just going to be there for ten minutes after all), and will mean you get to benefit from it much more quickly too.

You could choose an outside space, like a summer house or shed, but consider your location – will your use of the calm corner be dependent on weather conditions?

HOW TO CREATE A FEELING OF CALM

Make it comfy

Whatever kind of seat you have in your corner, make it snug and cocoon-like with a throw, blanket or cushion. Soft fabrics and a bit of padding can make even the most sturdy and plain chair or hard floor feel cozy and comforting, plus you can wrap yourself up to keep warm.

Find a light source

Having a nearby source of light, rather than switching on the "main light", makes it easier to read, write or craft, and adds to the intimate vibe we're going for. If your corner is by a window, you'll have the added benefit of natural light, as well as being able to gaze out at the sky and open a window when you're in need of a breeze.

Include a surface

You can use a table, bookshelf or window sill or, if that's not possible, find a box or basket instead. As well as being practical for holding your glass of water or cup of tea, you can use the surface to display items in your corner that bring you calm and joy.

Ideas for calm corner items

- Photo of your loved ones
- Book (in physical form)
- Candle
- Notebook and pen
- Plant
- Personal mementos
- Crystals
- Incense or essential oil diffuser/burner
- Craft project
- Jigsaw or puzzle

Choose items that promote calm and peace within you, not productivity or tasks to tick off your list.

No digital devices

The whole point of taking time to sit in your calm corner is to get some respite from the world – to have a place to be quiet, relax and recharge. Watching TV, checking emails or scrolling social media is not conducive to that! However, if you would like to listen to a guided meditation in your homemade sanctuary or to soothing music, start it playing and then put your device out of reach so you aren't tempted to pick it up again

MAKING USE OF YOUR CALM CORNER

For today's experiment, take ten minutes to design your calm corner. Then, it is ready and available to you whenever you're in need of a bit of quiet, alone time and the chance to catch your breath.

As well as experimenting with creating your calm corner, you can experiment with *when* you spend time in it and for how long. Do you find it most beneficial to begin or end your day there? At what times do you feel most in need of the comfort and calm it provides?

Your calm corner is yours to arrange and enjoy however and whenever you choose. And remember to let everyone in the household know that when you're in your calm corner you're off limits!

TAKEAWAY

My calm corner is my sanctuary.

EXPERIMENT 24

CREATE YOUR OWN POSITIVE AFFIRMATIONS

In this experiment, you're going to create one, or more, affirmations to give yourself positive messages.

WHAT IS AN AFFIRMATION?

An affirmation is a shorthand way of describing a statement that affirms a belief – which means affirmations aren't always positive. These statements are messages about ourselves that we may wholeheartedly *believe*, but may not actually be *true*.

However, because they are what we tell ourselves, over and over, they soak into us and we come to believe them to be true.

If you keep telling yourself a negative message such as, "I'm no good at running" or "I'm terrible at speaking in public", this is a negative affirmation that you will believe.

Affirmations aren't new to us, we use them all the time, we just may not recognize them as affirmations. By intentionally creating and using *positive* affirmations, you can give yourself messages of encouragement and support to build your confidence and self-belief.

THE DIFFERENCE BETWEEN AN AFFIRMATION AND A MANTRA

The words affirmation and mantra are often used interchangeably, but they aren't exactly the same. Mantra is a Hindu word defined as "a word or formula chanted or sung as an incantation or prayer".[1] An example of a mantra is when you repeat the word "breathe" to yourself over and over to remind yourself to breathe slowly and deeply to calm yourself.

In contrast, an affirmation is "a statement or proposition that is declared to be true".[2] In the context of this experiment, an affirmation is a present tense, first person, positive statement. Let me explain.

WHAT MAKES UP AN AFFIRMATION

There are three ingredients an affirmation – or statement of belief, as it could also be called – needs to maximize its power:

1. Being in the first person and in the present

An affirmation begins with "I am", "I can", "I have" or "I feel". Using "I will" or "I'm going to" puts the statement in the future, and we want you to be affirming a belief as true right now!

2. Being positive

This means you need to be sure a negative disguised as a positive isn't sneaking in. For example, "I am not as stressed as yesterday" or "I'm not scared" may sound sort of positive, but your brain is hearing the words "stressed" and "scared" and so affirms those words in your head. More powerful and positive affirmations would be "I feel relaxed today" or "I am brave". Now your brain is hearing the words "relaxed" and "brave", which is how you want to feel, and so is driving home that supportive message.

3. Feeling like it's possible for you

An outlandish, roll-your-eyes, out of this world crazy affirmation will be pretty ineffective as you're not going to believe it. For example, if you're lacking in confidence, an affirmation such as, "I am the most confident person in the world ever" may feel so out of reach that you can't believe in it at all. We want the affirmation to empower you, to help and support you, and while one day you may indeed be the most confident person in the world ever, right now that might feel absurd and totally unbelievable. A more supportive statement that may feel like a bit of stretch but ultimately possible could be, "I am growing in confidence every day". This statement is in the first person, in the present tense, positive and, while you may not feel very confident right now, this affirmation makes it feel like being confident *is* possible for you – you *can* grow in confidence every day.

Your affirmation doesn't have a word limit, you just want to be able to remember it and for it to feel empowering. It could be short, such as, "I am calm", or longer, such as, "I am honouring my needs and boundaries more and more every day".

USING YOUR AFFIRMATION

You may now realize you've been affirming beliefs to yourself for years – but often negative ones. Making use of positive affirmations requires a little more intention and conscious effort.

You can create several affirmations to pick and choose from depending on how you're feeling, the situation you're in or what you feel would be most supportive on any given day.

Here are some ideas for how to blend your affirmations into daily life:

- Write your affirmations on Post-it notes and stick them around your home so you're reminded of them throughout the day.
- Use your affirmation as a log-in password (if it's fairly short).
- Make your affirmation into an image and save it as your desktop picture or lock screen image on your mobile phone.
- Create a piece of art to represent your affirmation and put it on your wall.
- Write out your affirmations at the top of your diary or journal at the start or end of each day.
- Repeat your affirmation to yourself in bed as you drift off to sleep.
- Repeat your affirmation to yourself in bed when you wake up in the morning.
- Repeat your affirmation in your head while you do a specific daily task, such as making a cup of tea.
- Use a prompt, such as opening the door to your home or car: touching the handle is the nudge to repeat your affirmation (see Experiment 31, Make it a Habit).

POSITIVE POWER

Affirmations aren't magic, they're simply statements of belief, but they can be powerful and have a real impact on how you think and feel. Think about how powerful affirming a negative or critical belief about yourself is, how it impacts what you think, feel and do; so why not use this same power positively to help, support and encourage yourself.

Here are some examples of unhelpful belief statements you may have inadvertently been affirming, and some more supportive alternatives:

Negative	Positive
There's never enough time	*I have all the time I need*
I'm too tired	*I have all the energy I need*
Aargh, stressed!	*I am calm and collected*
I can't do it	*I can do this*
I should be better	*I am enough just as I am*
Everyone else is doing better than me	*I am running my own race*
I'm scared	*I am brave*
I don't know what I'm doing	*I can figure it out*
I'm such a failure	*I'm learning every day*

So, what do you want to believe about yourself today? What would be reassuring, supportive or encouraging?

TAKEAWAY

I am what I believe.

EXPERIMENT 25

DO "FUTURE YOU" A FAVOUR

For this experiment, we're going to spend ten minutes today that will take the pressure off you tomorrow. Because every day you make a *lot* of decisions – tiny little decisions, as well as big ones – and each one takes time, energy and brainpower. In fact, research by Cornell University[1] found that, although we might think we only make around 14 decisions a day about food (such as what, when, where, how much and with whom to eat) we actually make more like 226 decisions about food alone, each day!

And what about all the other decisions you're faced with daily? Choices such as what to wear, when to leave the house, where to go, what to watch or read, what to say and to whom, how and when to say it…

These are just a few of the decisions we make every day, and each one contains many more choices that need to be made within it.

Imagine walking along a busy street – you're required to make decisions constantly about where to walk and at what pace to avoid walking into people or street furniture, about which shop to go in, when and for what…

CHOICE OVERLOAD

Each choice and decision we make takes thinking power, or cognitive resources, which saps our energy little by little. And when we're faced with several choices, that can make decisions even harder, leading to analysis paralysis and decision fatigue (when specific names have been invented, you know it's a real thing). When there are lots of options available to us, we find it harder to make a decision; not just because of all the choices but also because of FOMO – the Fear Of Missing Out on a better choice we could or should have made.

We've all experienced sitting down at the end of the day ready to watch something on television and an hour later a decision still hasn't been reached because there are *so* many channels and streaming services with *so* many programmes and films on offer.

There's a famous study[2] that demonstrates how off-putting too many choices can be. Researchers set up a jam-tasting booth at a supermarket in California where every hour the selection of jams on offer changed from 6 flavours to 24 flavours. Most people chose to sample only one or two different types of jam, whether they were presented with 6 or 24. What's interesting is that 30 per cent of the customers who visited the booth when six flavours of jam were on offer bought a jar, but only 3 per cent of those who had the choice of 24 flavours went on to purchase. The fewer the options, the more likely it was that the customer reached a decision and took home a jar of jam.

Each decision we have to make is accompanied by a little dose of stress, because we have to weigh up our options, make a decision and hope it's the right one. Multiply this by all the decisions we make each day in our home and work lives and you can see the impact it can have.

EASE THE STRESS OF TOMORROW

There are plenty of decisions we can't make in advance, but by identifying the choices we *can* take ahead of time we save ourselves the brain ache and accompanying stress. And future you will thank you for it.

When he was President of the United States, Barack Obama told *Vanity Fair* that wearing only blue or grey suits helped him to cut down on the decisions he had to make each day.[3] You don't have to restrict your wardrobe in the same way, but he has a point about reducing the choices in each day.

If you think back over the last few days, there will have been times when you wished you had already made a decision but instead you were unsure what to do, feeling stuck or rushed, and making a choice was just another added stress.

For this experiment, you're going to take ten minutes to make some choices for tomorrow. Take a look at the list below and pick one to do now. (I realize that's another decision you have to make, but there's a choice because not all of them may be relevant.) If you have time leftover to make another decision, great!

Specifically for tomorrow

- Choose your outfit, iron it if needed, and hang the items together.
- Decide what's for dinner, check you have the ingredients or make a shopping list if not.
- Plan meals for the next week and make a shopping list.
- Prepare lunch and have it ready to pick up from the fridge.

- Look at the books in your to-be-read pile, choose one and put the rest away for now.
- Lay the table for breakfast (apart from refrigerated items, obviously).
- Pack your bag – handbag, work bag, gym bag – so it's ready to go.
- If you have a social event planned where a choice will need to be made – e.g. which restaurant, pub, cinema or film – decide on your preference now.

These are ideas to get you going on taking action that future you will thank you for. If you think of something else that's particular to your life, please do make a decision on that. You can see how you feel tomorrow about the choice you took today. You might find the experiment works so well you want to make it a regular habit!

TAKEAWAY

Future me appreciates what I do today.

EXPERIMENT 26

CREATE A SLEEP ROUTINE

Although this experiment is about sleep, it's not about getting you off to sleep now, or within ten minutes! This is a forward-planning experiment; spending ten minutes now to consider your current sleep routine and see how you can improve it, will result in you getting a better-quality night's sleep for a long time to come.

This book's strategy is based on utilizing 1% of your waking day to improve your overall wellbeing. When you subtract the recommended average of eight hours' sleep a day for adults,[1] 1% equals almost ten minutes. For some people, seven hours' sleep might be plenty, while others need more like nine hours. Do you sleep the number of hours you need to feel at your best?

But it's not only the number of hours you spend sleeping that matters, it's the *quality* of your sleep too.

WHY IS SLEEP IMPORTANT?

When you're busy or stressed, sleep is often one of the first casualties. Either you stay up later or get up earlier, so there's less time available for sleep; or your quality of sleep is eroded by a racing mind that's hard to switch off. As one can just about function on a bad night's sleep, there's a belief that it's something that can be sacrificed.

However, evidence shows this is not the case. Research published in *Nature and Science of Sleep*[2] shows that, in the short term, a lack of enough, quality sleep increases stress and emotional distress, negatively affects your mood, memory and cognitive functioning, and reduces your quality of life. Long-term consequences for otherwise healthy people can include cardiovascular disease, weight-related issues, Type 2 diabetes and even cancer. Sobering stuff.

Even without the scientific studies, you know yourself what difference it makes when you've had a good night's sleep compared to when you've had a shortened, disrupted night. It can affect how you feel, your mood, how clearly you can think and problem solve, your sense of humour, your energy, your appetite. In turn, that affects your relationships, your work, and how hard or joyful you find life.

ESTABLISHING A BEDTIME ROUTINE

It's clear that sleep is not a "nice-to-have" thing, it's *essential* for your wellbeing. And the best way to set yourself up for a good night's sleep is to create a sleep routine.

A bedtime routine might be something you associate with children – bath, pyjamas, brush teeth, into bed with a storybook, sleep. There's a reason parents follow the same pattern every evening: it's so their children's bodies and brains learn that it's time to wind down, relax and prepare for sleep.

As the children get older, the routine changes and eventually vanishes altogether. What does your nightly routine, if you have one, look like?

As adults with a lot on our plates, we can be working, doing housework or checking social media right up until we get into bed (or even while in bed) and turn out the lights, expecting and hoping to fall fast asleep instantly. It's a big ask. If you're physically worn out, you may crash out from exhaustion, but your mind may wake you up with random thoughts in the small hours. Or does your brain go into overdrive as soon as the light's switched off, and however much you will yourself to sleep, there are too many thoughts spinning round your head?

A sleep routine isn't just for children, anyone of any age can benefit from slowing down and training your body and brain to relax before bed. So, take these ten minutes to consider how you can experiment with your bedtime routine and what you want to try before bed tonight.

FIVE BEDTIME ROUTINE IDEAS

1. Set a deadline

If work creeps into your evenings, create an end to your busy day by deciding that if you haven't finished by a specific time it's not happening until the next day. Or perhaps choose a cut-off time for phone calls with friends and family; let them know that you're happy to chat any time up to 9pm, for example, but after that time your policy (see Experiment 13, Say "No" (Without Feeling Guilty)) is no more calls. You can even use the Do Not Disturb setting on your phone so you won't be bothered by pings.

2. Lower the lights

The human body's circadian rhythms respond to light and dark. When we're exposed to light, particularly bright light from digital screens,[3] our levels of the sleep hormone melatonin decrease. When light levels drop and it gets darker, melatonin production increases, making us feel sleepy.[4] By lowering the lights in your home toward the end of the evening *and* setting aside your screens well ahead of bedtime, you're giving your body the chance to release melatonin, which will help you get a good night's sleep. Televisions, mobile phones, tablets, laptops and games consoles all emit blue light, so choosing a cut-off time for these devices at least 30–60 minutes before you want to fall asleep would be a powerful part of your sleep routine.

3. Write it out

If you find yourself thinking a lot in bed, ruminating on the past and thinking about the future, a useful tool can be to write out whatever's in your head before bed. Just spill it all out onto paper, it doesn't have to be neat or spelt perfectly; what's important is that you get everything in your head down on paper so that you don't have to hold it in your brain any longer. (See Experiment 30, Try Freestyle Journaling.) Trying to plan, remember or figure out problems can keep you awake, and in the process of writing, a solution may appear; or you go to sleep knowing that you can come back to it the next day with a fresh head and new perspective.

4. Have a warm bath

Take a bath or shower, whichever you prefer. Not only does the warm water soothe and relax your muscles, which may be tight after a long day, it also increases your circulation, drawing heat from the core of your body to your hands and feet. Then, when you step out of the bathroom and head into the cooler bedroom, the slight (but significant) drop in body temperature acts as a wind down signal to your body. A study at the Harvard T.H. Chan School of Public Health found that taking a warm bath or shower one to two hours before bed can help you fall asleep ten minutes quicker.[5]

5. Do a calming activity

What would you find to be a calming, soothing, winding down activity before bed? Perhaps it's following a relaxing yoga video, meditating, using a mindfulness colouring book, or reading (but don't choose reading matter that's going to get your brain whirring). Maybe applying skin lotion, hand cream or giving yourself a foot massage would not only help you relax, but also feel like you're giving yourself some love, care and attention.

KEEP EXPERIMENTING

Try out different timings and different actions in different orders to see what feels good. What works for your friend or partner may be different to what works for you. It may take time for your sleep quality to change, so keep going and remember the theory of marginal gains – incremental changes with big results. This is your chance to begin creating a beautifully supportive bedtime ritual that will help you to have longer, deeper, better sleep in the long term.

Making sure your bedroom is dark, quiet and cool all contribute to better quality sleep, but taking ten minutes now to focus on your sleep routine (what you will do *before* heading to bed) will maximize your chances of a good night's sleep.

So, what are you going to experiment with as you get ready for bed tonight to set yourself up for a better night's sleep?

TAKEAWAY

Sleep is essential, not optional.

EXPERIMENT 27

END THE DAY WITH A "DONE" LIST

To Do lists can be great for focusing your mind and reminding you what you need to do and want to do. A To Do list means you don't have to try to keep everything in your head, and ticking items off as they're completed gives you a rewarding sense of accomplishment.

At the same time, however, an un-ticked list can be a powerful tool to beat yourself up with; you may take it as proof of how little you've done, how unproductive you've been and therefore how lazy, distracted and downright useless you are.

THE NEVER-ENDING LIST

When you think about it, a To Do list is never done. Even if what you have written down is all ticked off, you know there are more jobs that never made it on to the list. Depending on how the tasks are listed, it may be impossible to tick off something for several days. For example, "Finish project" may involve many hours of research, collaboration with colleagues, writing, editing... there can be a lot of work to complete before you can tick off those two innocent-looking words.

Then there may be other items that can never be completed, such as an open-ended entry like "Answer emails". Unless you plan to disconnect yourself from email forever more, this is a task that will never, ever be completely finished. However, the To Do list task "Answer email from Sam", for example, is finite and eminently tick off-able.

To Do lists keep us in busy, productive mode. While there is a need to be productive – we've all got stuff to do to pay the bills, have food to eat and clothes to wear – if you judge the quality of your day by the quantity of your output, you're setting yourself up to fail – especially if the only things on your To Do list are work-related.

So, for this experiment, let's try something different.

"WHOLE LIFE DONE" LIST

You may have heard of an alternative to a To Do list which is a Ta Da list – a record of all that you've achieved by the end of a day. Although it's a celebration of what you've accomplished (often focused on work or what you consider to be "good enough" to note down), it still plays into the pressure to be productive and tying that into your worth. If you don't have many items written on your Ta Da list, you may wonder what that says about how "good" a day you've had, or what it says about *you*.

Instead, we're going to experiment with writing a "Whole Life Done" list.

In a Whole Life Done list you include *everything*, not just what you've done at work or what you've done that *you* consider worthy of inclusion. Your Whole Life Done List includes *everything you've done*, from all areas of your life, that isn't part of your daily routine (so, you don't need to write "Got up, got dressed, had a shower", etc. – although you certainly can if it felt like an achievement!).

What you can include
What you choose to write on your Whole Life Done List is up to you. No one can tell you what counts or what's "good enough" to be written down – if it's something you want to include, just pop it on the list!

Here are some examples of what could feature in your Whole Life Done List:

- *Phoned my friend for a quick chat.*
- *Listened to the birds in my garden.*
- *Sent the email I'd been putting off.*
- *Read a chapter of my book while eating lunch.*
- *Finished the first draft of my presentation.*
- *Picked up my partner's dry cleaning.*
- *Found two useful pieces of research.*
- *Noticed some flower buds in the park have started blooming.*
- *Chatted with a neighbour while out for a walk.*
- *Swept the leaves from the driveway.*
- *Sent a card to my niece.*
- *Snuggled with the dog.*
- *Tried a new recipe for dinner.*
- *Meditated.*
- *Let someone go ahead of me in the checkout queue.*

The list could go on and on, but you get the idea.

None of these items are particularly exciting, they're not grand achievements, but they do represent the whole of you and your day, not just the shiny parts.

WHY WRITE A WHOLE LIFE DONE LIST?

Writing a list like this appeases the need to feel productive, but that's only part of it. The Whole Life Done List helps you to keep a more rounded perspective of your life – it's not just about how much work you accomplish, it's what happens in your whole life. It shows that your day (and lives are made up of days, after all) has moments of self-care, connection, curiosity, peace, awe, joy…

By listing the range of what you do in a day, you can see how you've spent time doing what helps you to be healthy, what strengthens your relationships, what gives you fulfilment, calm, energy, joy.

Or not…

What's missing from your list?

If you look over your Whole Life Done List and it's lacking the kinds of actions that make you feel good and fill your metaphorical cup, that's valuable information too. It shows where you may be neglecting your own needs or desires, how you may be out of kilter with what feels nourishing for you, thereby offering an explanation for why you may not be feeling as good as you'd like to.

Writing a Whole Life Done List may sound too simple to really make much of a difference. But, if you only focus on what you deem to have been "productive", if that's how you judge the value of your day (or yourself), your thinking and feeling is going to be through that lens. Writing a Whole Life Done List allows you to focus on the rounded human being that you are.

Science writer Winifred Gallagher wrote, "Who you are, what you think, feel, and do, what you love – is the sum of what you focus on."[1] And I agree.

TAKEAWAY

My whole life is valuable.

PUT ON YOUR PROTECTIVE ONESIE

Do any of the following statements ring a bell with you?

- While watching a gripping TV show, you really feel what the characters are going through.
- You avoid watching the news because seeing violence and suffering can feel too distressing.
- You don't like watching scary films because you feel the anxiety and fear of the characters, almost as if you're them.
- Being around someone who's grumpy, finding fault or very pessimistic puts you in the same mood too.
- You're told you're a good listener, and are often asked for advice.
- When a friend is happy and excited about something you can't help but feel that joy too.
- When a friend is upset you feel their sadness almost as if it's yours.

- It feels instinctive to help when you see another person struggling.
- You understand what someone is trying to say even if they're having trouble communicating it – you get where they're coming from.
- You can spot when someone's lying or if they're hiding something.
- You pick up the feel or vibe of a room quickly, even if you don't know the people there.

If you're nodding along to several of these statements, you're most likely a highly empathetic person. Nick Trenton, author of *The Empath Self-care Blueprint*, describes an empath as "a person with a heightened capacity for empathy, or someone with the ability to feel the emotions of others. Rather than merely understanding another person's state of mind on an intellectual level, empaths seem to 'let more in', and can find themselves literally feeling the emotional reality of another person." [1]

Let's be clear, being an empath is not some kind of diagnosed condition; it's merely a term that can be useful in describing and understanding a natural trait. Being highly empathetic is not a flaw or failing. It's not because you're *too* sensitive or you should have a thicker skin (although you've probably been told both many times); it's because part of your nature is to be able to connect deeply with people on an emotional level. This can mean that, as an empath, you're processing a lot of extra information, which, at times, can feel exhausting and overwhelming. You might wish that you didn't feel so deeply, or that you find intense conversations so draining, that you could somehow switch off your emotional antennae because it can feel like such a rollercoaster!

And this is why you're going to experiment with a technique to help maintain your equilibrium.

ACCEPT YOUR EMPATHIC NATURE

Knowing about your high empathy and how it can impact your energy and emotions is very useful for a couple of reasons:

1. You now have an explanation for why it can seem like your mood and emotions are dependent on the people around you.
2. You can now identify what's contributing to feelings of overwhelm.

With this knowledge, you can take action to better protect yourself from being overpowered by emotions.

PROTECT YOUR EMOTIONS

One way to look after your wellbeing is through creating, communicating and honouring your boundaries (see Experiment 4, Create a Personal Boundary). For example, if watching the news feels overwhelmingly distressing, perhaps choose to *listen* to the news on the radio instead, or to only catch up with the news once a day. Another example is that before offering to help a friend who's struggling, pause to consider what resources (energy, time, finances, emotional strength) you have to give.

One other way – and this is what this experiment is all about – is to put on your protective onesie (metaphorically). There are some people in our lives who can really impact how we feel (and not in a good way) but whom we can't simply cut out of our lives. A protective onesie comes in particularly handy for encounters with those folk, as well as for any situation or conversation where we can feel our emotions being swept away.

Put on your protective onesie

To put on your protective onesie, you have to imagine you're wearing an invisible all-in-one outfit – a onesie or a jumpsuit that fits close to your skin or is puffed up like the Michelin man – however you like to visualize it. And you're not the only one wearing a protective onesie, everyone else in the world is wearing their own invisible all-in-one too. Everything about an individual is contained within this suit. You get to choose what stays inside the invisible layer, what can pass through from you to the outer environment, and what does and does not come in from the outside world.

Imagine you're talking to someone and you can feel their fear, their stress, their anxiety, their sadness (or whatever their emotions are) pouring out of them and flowing toward you. With your invisible protective onesie on you can acknowledge their struggle, empathize with them, give them kindness and compassion, offer them support (if you're able to), but their strong feelings don't pass through your invisible layer and into you, meaning you don't take on their emotions as your own.

Protection not disconnection

This is not about making you less empathetic; it's about helping you to identify which emotions are yours and which belong to others, and to not be overwhelmed by them.

This invisible layer doesn't stop you from connecting to another person. It doesn't put up a wall or make you uncaring or unfeeling. It gives you whatever level of protection you want to keep your emotions from being overwhelmed by other people or your environment. It's your choice how permeable you want your invisible onesie to be at any given moment. If you want to take on the energy and emotions of your friend who's fizzing with excitement, you're completely free to do that; but if you want to protect yourself from being overwhelmed by another friend's grief (while still being your caring self), you can do that too.

TRY IT ON FOR YOURSELF

For this ten-minute experiment, imagine what your invisible protective onesie or jumpsuit looks like, what it's made of and how it feels to wear it.

Visualize yourself in your suit walking into a room of people, or while you watch TV or while sitting in conversation with someone.

Think about the situations and people in your life with whom you will feel more comfortable, stronger and safer wearing your invisible protective onesie.

If there's an opportunity where you can put wearing your invisible suit into practice, all the better! Notice how it feels to imagine you're wearing it while in the situation, and how you feel afterwards.

TAKEAWAY

I'm wearing my invisible protective onesie.

EXPERIMENT 29

GIVE YOURSELF PERMISSION

For this experiment, we're going to explore how we can give ourselves more "permission", because it's something that many of us struggle a lot with in life. There's stuff that we just don't feel we can do, that we don't feel we're allowed to do or allowed to not do, Or to feel what we're feeling, Or to think what we're thinking. Or to say what we want to say. Or to be who we want to be.

Maybe you tell yourself you shouldn't be fed up because other people have it harder than you. Perhaps you curb your excitement over some good news because you don't want to seem self-centred. Maybe you continue reading a book you're not enjoying because it seems wrong to stop before the end. Or perhaps you say yes to doing something, even though you really wanted to say no (see Experiment 13, Say "No" (Without Feeling Guilty)).

You might not be fully aware you're holding yourself back, not allowing yourself; but on a deeper level you'll know, because you feel uncomfortable, it feels heavy or onerous or something just feels off – you feel more stressed, perhaps some overwhelm, and a feeling of not being in control of your life.

LOOKING ELSEWHERE FOR PERMISSION

As children we learn to seek permission from parents and teachers, and as adults we can find ourselves looking to authority figures like our bosses or doctors, strangers and celebrities on social media, as well as our friends and loved ones, to make us feel like we have permission.

Seeking permission can look like:

- sighing loudly about how tired you are in the hope your partner suggests you take a long bath and get an early night
- remarking to your boss how interesting the new project sounds in the hope she suggests you work on it, because you don't think you should ask outright
- telling your friend you shouldn't have a slice of cake with your coffee in the hope she suggests you treat yourself

- complaining to your flatmate about how much work you've brought home in the hope they'll suggest getting a takeaway for dinner, even though it's your turn to cook.

You can get so used to looking for external approval that you find it difficult to give yourself approval. Plus, you might find it hard to give yourself permission because you're busy taking care of everyone else – you're used to being the responsible person who looks after everyone else's needs. You want to make everyone happy, keep the peace, be a good person and get everyone's approval.

But all of this holding yourself back, denying your feelings, biting your tongue, taking on unwanted tasks or responsibilities takes up your time, energy and brainpower.

While there is a bigger issue of challenging and changing the societal structures that have systematically created obstructions to feeling you deserve and can give yourself permission for what you want and need, there is still one small, and powerful, personal action you can take in just ten minutes: permission slips.

GIVE YOURSELF PERMISSION

Writing yourself a permission slip can feel strange if it's not something you're used to doing, but it's also pretty empowering because you're giving yourself, in your own words, what you most need.

Your permission slip can be broad, such as, "I give myself permission to make mistakes" or "I'm allowed to give my opinion", or very specific, such as, "I give myself permission to leave the dishes until I've had a cup of coffee" or "I'm allowed to not like mushrooms even if the rest of my family think I'm weird". Remember this is about freeing *yourself*; so, give yourself permission for what you really want or need, not what you think you should be or do.

Here are a few suggestions to get you thinking about what permission slips you want:

- *I give myself permission to rest.*
- *I'm allowed to disagree with other people.*
- *I give myself permission to take my time.*
- *I'm allowed to be proud of myself.*
- *I give myself permission to ignore my To Do list.*
- *I'm allowed to change my mind.*

- *I give myself permission to follow my intuition.*
- *I'm allowed to feel sad/angry/nervous/excited.*

Making your permission slips

While you could just say the permission to yourself or make a note in your phone, a more fun (and impactful) method is to make actual permission slips (like you may have had at school) from individual pieces of card or paper.

Take ten minutes to make your permission slips and keep the stack somewhere handy, so that you can either pick one at random when you want to stretch your self-permission muscle or pull out the specific one you need in that moment.

TAKEAWAY

I give myself permission.

EXPERIMENT 30

TRY FREESTYLE
JOURNALING

In recent years, journaling has become increasingly popular. At first glance, it may seem like a laborious activity that requires a beautifully bound notebook and fancy fountain pen in Insta-worthy surroundings. That's what social media might have you believe anyway. Gone are the days when you scribbled down your thoughts and feelings, hopes and plans in a notebook or diary — now you "journal" in a journal (yes, it's a verb and a noun).

But swipe away the Pinterest-perfect picture, and journaling is still what it always has been — a way to write out your inner world. Through writing down what's in your head, whether or not you follow a particular system or prompts, you can work through problems, birth ideas, make plans, bring dreams to life, explore your feelings or simply unload your angst.

It may have been something you did as a teenager in an attempt to make sense of the confusing world you and your hormones were trying to navigate, but as an adult it's fallen by the wayside.

We've looked at other forms of writing experiments (see Experiment 5, Conjure up Your Best Future Self; Experiment 11, Keep a Gratitude Journal; Experiment 20, Uncover Your Inner Strength) which are all distinctly different to each other – and this experiment in journaling is completely different again. For your experiment today, you're going to have a go at freestyle journaling.

FREESTYLE JOURNALING

Essentially, freestyle journaling is spilling the contents of your mind onto paper. You write everything down, without worrying about neat handwriting or grammatical rules – just get your thoughts down on paper as a stream of consciousness. There are no specific prompts to follow, no set questions to answer, no guidelines to stay within. You just empty out all that's spinning around your head through pen onto paper.

It's freestyle because there are no rules. It doesn't matter what you write in or on – it can be a beautiful journal, an old notepad or the back of an envelope. It doesn't matter if your writing is scrawly and wobbly, if your spelling is off, or if your sentences run on for half a page non-stop. There's no minimum or maximum word or page count – you don't even have to write for the full experimental ten minutes if that stresses you out!

You can choose whether to throw away your writing as soon as you're done, re-read it straight away, or keep it in a drawer with the option to look back on it at a later point. If the thought of reading it back has the effect of self-censoring (because of potential self-judgement) allow yourself to tear it up as soon as you finish. On the flipside, if you want to read back through your written thoughts because you think that could help, you can do that too.

FIND CLARITY AND PERSPECTIVE

Because the process of writing slows down your thinking (you can't write as quickly as you can think), journaling means you can see your thoughts more clearly. Just like if you say something out loud, you hear it more clearly than if you just say it in your head.

By reading back over your writing, you might see that what was perhaps feeling scary or difficult is not actually as big a deal as you originally thought. It may not be that worrisome or as daunting now that you see it written down.

In the process of writing out what's in your head – your worries, fears, To Do list, past conversations – you might gain a different perspective, see them in a different light, because you're looking at your thoughts with a little distance instead of being caught up in them whirring through your brain.

You might realize what's really important – what you want to focus on or what you can let go of. New ideas can spring to mind, solutions or a different way forward. Maybe you gained insight or clarity from the process, and maybe you didn't – that's okay.

CREATE CALM AND PEACE

Sometimes emptying your head onto a piece of paper simply provides release and relief. You've vented, you've let it out in a way that feels private, safe.

So, take your ten minutes experiment time to empty your head onto a piece of paper and compare how you feel afterwards with how you felt before.

It's your writing, your journaling – you're freestyling.

MORNING PAGES

Julia Cameron, author of *The Artist's Way*, believes that starting each day with writing three pages of whatever's in your head frees up your creativity because it clears out the "angry, whiny, petty stuff".[1] She suggests you write out your thoughts as you have them, however random they are; for example, "I don't know what to write... what was that noise... must remember to get broccoli for dinner...". And then to put them aside and not read them (at least for the first eight weeks if you do this daily).

TAKEAWAY

I can create space and peace in my mind.

EXPERIMENT 31

MAKE IT A HABIT

There may be actions or tasks that you do that you'd love to make a regular part of your day, to make them a habit. And some of the experiments you'll discover in this book may make such an impact on you that you'll want to embed them in your life, perhaps practising them every day. So, what's a good way to blend these actions into your life and make them habitual?

This is what we're exploring in our final experiment!

There are many different ways to form a habit – whole books have been written solely focusing on this one challenge. For this experiment, we're going to focus on just one technique, and it's one that I have found most helpful – habit stacking.

Thought to have originated by American social scientist and author B J Fogg (he calls it anchoring[1]), habit stacking is what it sounds like: you stack habits together.

WHY HABIT STACK?

Trying to establish a brand-new activity in your life on a regular basis can be pretty tricky. In a busy life, it's not easy to remember to do something new daily, even if you really want to do it, because your brain is chock-a-block remembering lots of other stuff.

When you repeat an action over and over again, connections are made between the neurons in your brain. These connections, known as synapses, get stronger the more often you repeat the action. Perform an act haphazardly and the synapses remain weak; don't do it for a long time and the connection is pruned away. It's the strong synapses that make it easy for you to repeat an action over and over, without really thinking about it. Like opening the bedroom curtains when you've finished getting dressed in the morning, or brushing your teeth before you get into bed at night.

You already have many well-established habits in your daily life, so make use of them to bed in a new habit by stacking the new wished-for habit with the ingrained habit.

Examples of daily habits
- Shower
- Brush your teeth
- Get dressed
- Make a cup of tea or coffee

- Feed the cat
- Walk the dog
- Drive to work
- Eat lunch
- Eat dinner
- Stack the dishwasher
- Watch the news
- Wash your face
- Change into pyjamas
- Read your book
- Turn lights out

HOW TO HABIT STACK

Decide on the new habit you want to establish; it needs to be a clearly defined action, such as "Do three sun salutations", not a vague wish, like "Do yoga". Then think about what habits you already have that you could stack it with.

For example, if you want to get into the habit of writing in your gratitude journal, decide to always do that straight after putting on your pyjamas. This means that to get into the habit of writing in your gratitude journal you don't need to think of when and where to do it each day. You've decided it's the action you take immediately after dressing for bed – which is already a constant in your routine. Stacking journaling with this particular daily habit works well because you have the day to look back on, and you can keep your journal to hand on your bedside table.

Another example could be that you want to introduce a ten-minute meditation into your day. Think about what time of day you'd like to meditate (I say "would like to" rather than "should" because you're much more likely to actually do the thing if it's out of choice rather than obligation). First thing in the morning to get your day off to a good start? At lunchtime to act as a reset button? In the evening as part of your wind-down routine?

When you've decided the point in your day you want to meditate, choose an action you already do every day at that time to stack it with. So, if you want to meditate in the morning, why not make it the action you take as soon as you finish your morning tea or coffee.

Habit sandwiching

To habit stack, you've decided that after you've done action x you'll do new action y. To ingrain it into your routine further, you could *habit sandwich*, where your new action is the sandwich filling. This looks like:

After I've done action x and before I do action z,
I'll do new action y.

For example:

> *After I've dropped the kids at school and before I get to the office, I'll take a ten-minute mindful walk.*

An alternative way to order this phrase which you might find helpful is:

> *After I've done action x, I'll do new action y, before I do action z.*

For example:

> *After I get in the car to drive home, I'll take ten slow breaths in and out, before I start the engine.*

Multi-habit stack

There are some habits, or perhaps "actions" is a more appropriate word here, that you do multiple times a day, such as use the toilet or wash your hands. If there's an action you want to get into the habit of doing several times a day, such as stretching out your shoulders, you could stack it with another repeated action; for example:

After every time I wash my hands, I will do five shoulder rolls.

HABIT STACK 1% EXPERIMENTS

Here are some examples of how you can make the experiments in this book into regular habits through habit stacking:

- *While I brush my teeth, I'll choose a mantra for the day.*
- *When I get home, I'll sit in my calm corner for ten minutes before I start making dinner.*
- *When I finish work, I'll take two minutes to write my Whole Life Done list before I put on my coat to leave.*
- *After I've eaten lunch, I'll take a mindful walk.*
- *When I let the dog out for the last time at night, I'll take five slow breaths in and out.*
- *When I sit down at my desk and before I switch on my computer, I'll repeat an affirmation to myself.*
- *After dinner, I'll make tomorrow's lunch before I wash up.*
- *Before I get out of bed, I'll name five things I'm looking forward to.*
- *After I get into bed and before I lie down, I'll meditate for ten minutes.*
- *After I load the dishwasher, I'll write in my gratitude journal.*

GO GENTLY ON YOURSELF

As with all of the experiments you've been exploring in this book, when you're trying to establish a new habit, go gently on yourself. It's highly unlikely that you'll do your chosen action every day without fail from the get-go. You're probably going to forget or skip a day, and that's okay – it doesn't mean that you'll never make it a habit; it just means that your synapses need to fire together more often to wire together. Just keep at it!

TAKEAWAY

Stacking habits makes them happen.

WHAT TO DO NEXT

You've reached the end of the 31 experiments in this book – so what next?

As I wrote at the start of this book, nothing – including the ideas shared here – is going to make your life super-shiny, perfect and easy-breezy. Because nothing in the world can do that and no one's life is like that. You may have found that not every experiment worked for you – and that's okay.

All too often, we can be quick to dismiss or forget progress we've already made in our haste to move on further, to tick off the next task, to reach the next goal. There's even a name for this: destination addiction.[1]

So, at this point in the experiment, let's take time to acknowledge and celebrate all those micro-gains you've clocked up.

Whether you tried all or just some of the ideas, whether you spent one calendar month or longer working your way through the experiments, the most important thing is that *you gave it a go*.

You've been open to trying out new ways of thinking and behaving, willing to change how you've been going about your days to discover what works for you and what will make a real difference to your wellbeing.

ALL THAT YOU'VE GAINED

Throughout the experiments, you may have had moments where you felt challenged or uncomfortable, had lightbulb moments and realizations, and discovered more about yourself than you perhaps expected when you turned the first page of this book. You've learned about mindfulness, meditation, self-compassion, people-pleasing, boundaries, CBT, expressive writing and much more. You've uncovered resources within yourself you may not have known you had.

You've discovered how long, or short, ten minutes or 1% of your day feels – and how much you can achieve in that time. Through experimenting, you've found how to transform your mood, lighten your load, strengthen your relationships, build your confidence and self-trust, save time, soothe and empower yourself.

And you're reaping the benefits.

WHERE YOU GO FROM HERE

With any experiment, you need to review your data. In this context, it means looking back at any notes you made during the experiments you tried, following the questions on pxxx in the Introduction. Turn back to the Keeping Track table on pxxxiv to see which experiments you loved and want to repeat, and which need a little tweaking before trying again.

Take a moment to reflect on your experimental month:

- Which experiments did you enjoy the most?
- Which challenged you?
- What new ideas for supporting your wellbeing have come to mind through exploring these experiments?

KEEP EXPERIMENTING

Capitalize on all the effort you've put in, all the experimenting you've done and keep going. Here are a few ideas to continue exploring the experiments:

- Repeat all the experiments you marked as "Repeat!"
- Work through your "Tweak & try again" list, and hone the experiments so they work for you.

- Try all the even numbered experiments.
- Try all the odd numbered experiments.
- Start at the end of the experiment list and work your way back to the start.
- Partner with a friend for a selection of experiments.
- Choose experiments you can conduct in your calm corner (Experiment 23) such as experiments 1, 9 and 30.
- If you want to work on challenging your people-pleasing tendency, try experiments 4, 13 or 29.
- If you want to work on staying out of the comparison trap, try experiments 11, 19 or 28.
- If you want life to feel calmer, try experiments 6, 14 or 25.
- If you want to strengthen your confidence, try experiments 8, 16 or 24.

Now you know what action you want to take forward, think about how you're going to do that: what form you want it to take, when, where and how you'll put it into practice.

Remember: what matters is that you find what works for *you*, and you can do this through experimenting, exploring, trying things out and tweaking.

PRACTICE MAKES PROGRESS

The benefits to your mental, emotional and physical health of these actions and tools come from practising them again and again. Rarely is there something in life that only has to be done once to have a meaningful, lasting, positive impact. Making the choice to honour your boundaries, to savour moments, to play, to focus on what's in your control, to take mindful walks... doing this over and over again repeatedly is where the gold lies.

And now you have built your own bespoke toolkit of actions that makes a powerful difference to your life and takes just 1% of your day. Congratulations!

REFERENCES

Introduction

1 Allen, E. (2014). *Sir Dave Brailsford at British Cycling – A career retrospective.* [online] Available at: https://www.britishcycling.org.uk/gbcyclingteam/article/gbr20140411-British-Cycling—The-Brailsford-years-0 [Accessed 18 January 2023].

2 Slater, M. (2008). *How GB cycling went from tragic to magic.* [online] Available at: http://news.bbc.co.uk/sport1/hi/olympics/cycling/7534073.stm [Accessed 18 January 2023].

3 Fordyce, T. (2017). *Tour de France 2017: Is Chris Froom Britain's least loved great sportsman?* [online] Available at: https://www.bbc.co.uk/sport/cycling/40692045 [Accessed 18 January 2023].

4 Lewis, T. (2019). *Golden aura around marginal gains is beginning to look a little tarnished.* [online] Available at: https://www.theguardian.com/sport/blog/2019/oct/20/marginal-gains-tarnished-bradley-wiggins-dave-brailsford [Accessed 18 January 2023].

5 Harrell, E. (2015). *How 1% performance improvements led to Olympic gold.* [online] Available at: https://hbr.org/2015/10/how-1-performance-improvements-led-to-olympic-gold [Accessed 18 January 2023].

6 Clear, J. (2018). *Atomic Habits.* Random House.

7 Fordyce, T. (2012). *Win puts Wiggins among Olympic greats.* [online] Available at: https://www.bbc.co.uk/blogs/tomfordyce/2012/07/wiggins_tour_win_ranks_among_b.html [Accessed 18 January 2023].

8 Bergland, C. (2018). *Is the perfectionism plague taking a psychological toll?* [online] Available at: https://www.psychologytoday.com/gb/blog/the-athletes-way/201801/is-the-perfectionism-plague-taking-psychological-toll [Accessed 12 June 2023].

9 Dr Seuss. (1990). *Oh, the Places You'll Go!*, HarperCollins.

Experiment 2

1 Neff, K. (2023). Self-compassion theory, method, research and intervention. *Annual Review of Psychology, 74*, 193–218.

2 Neff, K. (2003). Self-compassion: An alternative conceptualisation of a healthy attitude toward oneself. *Self and Identity, 2*, 85–101.

Experiment 3

1 Bhattacharaya, S., Bahar, M., & Singh, A. (2019). NOMOPHOBIA: NO Mobile Phone phobia. *Journal of Family Medicine and Primary Care, 8(4)*, 1297–1300.

2 Hennessy, S., Sachs, M., Kaplan, J., & Habibi, A. (2021). Music and mood regulation during the early stages of the COVID-19 pandemic. *PLoS ONE, 16(10)*, 1–17.

Experiment 4

1   American Psychological Association. [online] Available
    at: https://dictionary.apa.org/boundary [Accessed
    20 March 2023].
2   Therapist Aid. (2016). [online] Available at: https://uhs.
    berkeley.edu/sites/default/files/relationships_personal_
    boundaries.pdf [Accessed 20 March 2023].

Experiment 5

1   Sheldon, K. M. & Lyubomirsky, S. (2006). How to increase and
    sustain positive emotion: The effects of expressing gratitude
    and visualising best possible selves. *The Journal of Positive
    Psychology*, 1(2), 73–82.
2   King, L. A. (2001). The health benefits of writing about life goals.
    Personality and Social Psychology Bulletin, 27(7), 798–807.

Experiment 6

1   Stone, L. (2011). *Just breathe: Building the case for email
    apnea*. [online] Available at: https://www.huffpost.com/
    entry/just-breathe-building-the_b_85651 [Accessed
    1 February 2023].
2   American Psychological Association. (2018). *Stress effects on
    the body*. [online] Available at: https://www.apa.org/topics/
    stress/body [Accessed 1 February 2023].
3   Williams, C. (2020). *How to breathe your way to better memory
    and sleep*. [online] Available at: https://www.newscientist.com/
    article/mg24532640-600-how-to-breathe-your-way-to-better-
    memory-and-sleep/ [Accessed 1 February 2023].

4   Chen, Y., Huang, X., Chien, C., & Cheng, J. (2016). The effectiveness of diaphragmatic breathing relaxation training for reducing anxiety. *Perspectives in Psychiatric Care 53*(4), 329–336.

Experiment 7

1   Dunn, E., Aknin.L., & Norton, M. (2008). Spending money on others promotes happiness. *Science, 319*, 1687–1688.
2   Lyubomirky, S. & Della Porta, M. (2010). *Boosting happiness and buttressing resilience.* [online] Available at: http://sonjalyubomirsky.com/wp-content/themes/sonjalyubomirsky/papers/LDinpressb.pdf [Accessed 24 April 2023].
3   Otake, K., Shimai, S., Tanaka-Matsu, J., & Fredrickson, B. (2006). Happy people become happier through kindness: A counting kindness intervention. *Journal of Happiness Studies, 7*(3), 361–375.
4   Nook, E., Ong, D., Morelli, S., Mitchell, J., & Zaki, J. (2016). Prosocial conformity: Prosocial norms generalize across behavior and empathy. *Personality and Social Psychology Bulleting, 42*(8),1045–1062.

Experiment 8

1   Covey, S. (1989). *The 7 Habits of Highly Effective People.* Simon & Schuster.

Experiment 9

1   Hatano, A., Ogulmus, C., Shigemasu, H., & Murayama, K. (2022). Thinking about thinking: People underestimate how

enjoyable and engaging waiting is. *Journal of Experimental Psychology: General*, 1–17.

2 Baird, B., Smallwood, J., Mrazek, M., Kam, J., Franklin, M., & Schooler, J. (2012). Inspired by distraction: Mind wandering facilitates creative incubation. *Psychological Science, 23*(10), 1059–1271.

Experiment 11

1 Holden, R. (2011). *What is destination addiction?* [online] Available at: https://www.robertholden.com/blog/what-is-destination-addiction/ [Accessed 7 April 2023].

2 Emmons, R. (2013). *Gratitude Works! A 21 Day Program for Creating Emotional Prosperity.* Jossey Bass.

3 Brickman, P., Coates, D., & Janoff Bulman, R. (1978). Lottery winners and accident victims: Is happiness relative? *Journal of Personality and Social Psychology, 36*(8), 917–927.

4 Vaish, A., Grossmann, T., & Woodward, A. (2008). Not all emotions are created equal: the negativity bias in social-emotional development. *Psychological Bulletin, 134*(3), 383–403.

5 Hanson, R. *Take in the good.* [online] Available at: https://www.rickhanson.net/take-in-the-good [Accessed 7 April 2023].

6 Fredrickson, B., Tugade, M., Waugh, C., & Larkin, G. (2003). What good are positive emotions in crises? A prospective study of resilience and emotions following the terrorist attacks on the United States on September 11th. *Journal of Personality and Social Psychology, 84*(2), 365–376.

7 Emmons, R. & McCullough, M. (2003). Counting Blessings Versus Burdens: An Experimental Investigation of Gratitude

and Subjective Well-Being in Daily Life. *Journal of Personality and Social Psychology, 84*(2), 377–389.

8 Keita, U., Takuya, I., Takahiro, Y. & Kuniyoshi, L. (2021). Paper Notebooks vs. Mobile Devices: Brain Activation Differences During Memory Retrieval. *Frontiers in Behavioral Neuroscience*, Vol. 15, 1–11.

Experiment 12

1 Nash, J. (2019). *The history of meditation: Its origins and timeline.* [online] Available at: https://positivepsychology.com/history-of-meditation/ [Accessed 17 March 2023].

2 Goldin, P. & Gross, J. (2010). Effects of mindfulness-based stress reduction (MBSR) on emotion regulation in social anxiety disorder. *Emotion, 10*(1), 83–91.

3 Kabat-Zinn, J., Massion, A., Kristeller, J., Peterson, L., Fletcher, K., Pbert, L., Lenderking, W. & Santorelli, S. (1992). Effectiveness of a meditation-based stress reduction program in the treatment of anxiety disorders. *American Journal of Psychiatry, 149*(7), 936–943.

4 Rusch, H., Rosario, M., Levison, L., Olivera, A., Livingston, W., Wu, T., & Jessica M. (2019). The effect of mindfulness meditation on sleep quality: A systematic review and meta-analysis of randomized controlled trials. *Annals of the New York Academy of Sciences, 1445*(1), 5–16.

5 Zeidan, F., Johnson, S., Diamond, B., David, Z., & Goolkasian, P. (2010). Mindfulness meditation improves cognition: Evidence of brief mental training. *Consciousness and cognition, 19*(2), 597–605.

Experiment 14

1 Gotink, R., Hermans, K., Geschwind, N., De Nooij, R., De Groot, W., & Speckens, A. (2016). Mindfulness and mood stimulate each other in an upward spiral: a mindful walking intervention using experience sampling. *Mindfulness, 7*, 1114–1122.

2 Teut, M., Roesner, E., Ortiz, M., Reese, F., Binting. S., Roll. S., Fischer, H., Michalsen, A., Willich, S., & Brinkhaus, B. (2013). Mindful walking in psychologically distressed individuals: A randomized controlled trial. *Evidence-Based Complementary and Alternative Medicine, 13, 1–7.*

Experiment 16

1 Walker, T. (2014). Maya Angelou dies. 'You may encounter many defeats, but you must not be defeated'. [online] Available at: https://www.independent.co.uk/news/people/ maya-angelou-dies-you-may-encounter-many-defeats- but-you-must-not-be-defeated-9449234.html [Accessed 17 March 2023].

2 Marley, R. (1977). *Three Little Birds.* Island Records.

3 Jobs, S. (2005). Commencement address. Stanford University.

4 Hussain, N. (2015). *The Great British Bake Off.* Love Productions.

Experiment 17

1 McGowan, S., K. & Behar, E. (2013). A preliminary investigation of stimulus control training for worry: Effects on anxiety and insomnia. *Behavior Modification 37*(1), 90–112.

Experiment 18

1 Brown, B. (2010). *The Gifts of Imperfection: Let go of who you think you're supposed to be and embrace who you are.* Hazelden.

2 Umberson, D. & Montez, J. (2010). Social relationships and health: A flashpoint for health policy. *Journal of Health and Social Behavior, 51*(S), S54-S66.

3 Przybylski, A. & Weinstein, N. (2013). Can you connect with me now? How the presence of mobile communication technology influences face to face conversation quality. *Journal of Social and Personal Relationships, 30*(3), 237–246.

4 Uvnas-Moberg, K., Handlin, L., & Petersson, M. (2015). Self-soothing behaviors with particular reference to oxytocin release induced by non-noxious sensory stimulation. *Frontiers in Psychology, 5*(1), 1–16.

Experiment 19

1 Bryant, F. (2003). Savoring Beliefs Inventory (SBI): A scale for measuring beliefs about savouring. *Journal of Mental Health, 12*(2), 175–196.

2 Jose, P., Lim, B., & Bryan, T. (2012). Does savoring increase happiness? A daily diary study. *The Journal of Positive Psychology, 7*(3), 176–187.

3 Quoidbach, J., Dunn, E., Petrides, K., & Mikolajczak, M. (2010). Money giveth, money taketh away: The dual effect of wealth on happiness. *Psychological Science, 21*(6), 759–763.

Experiment 20

1　Glass, O., Dreusicke, M., Evans, J., Bechard, E., & Wolever, R. (2019). Expressive writing to improve resilience to trauma: A clinical feasibility trial. *Complementary Therapies in Clinical Practice, 34*, 240–246.

Experiment 21

1　Brown, S. (2010). *Play: How it shapes the brain, opens the imagination and invigorates the soul.* Penguin.

2　Proyer, R. (2013). The well-being of playful adults: Adult playfulness, subjective well-being, physical well-being and the pursuit of enjoyable activities. *European Journal of Humour Research 1(1)*, 84–98.

3　Magnuson, C. & Barnett, A. (2013). The playful advantage: How playfulness enhances coping with stress. *Leisure Sciences, 35(2)*, 129–144.

Experiment 24

1　Dictionary.com. *Mantra.* [online] Available at: https://www.dictionary.com/browse/mantra [Accessed 17 March 2023].

2　Dictionary.com. *Affirmation.* [online] Available at: https://www.dictionary.com/browse/affirmation [Accessed 17 March 2023].

Experiment 25

1 Wansink, B. & Sobal, J. (2007). Mindless eating: The 200 daily food decisions we overlook. *Environment and Behavior, 39*(1), 106–123.

2 Iyengar, S. & Lepper, M. (2000). When choice is demotivating: Can one desire too much of a good thing? *Journal of Personality and Social Psychology, 79*(6), 995–1006.

3 Lewis, M. (2012). *Obama's Way.* [online] Available at: https://www.vanityfair.com/news/2012/10/michael-lewis-profile-barack-obama [Accessed 24 April 2023].

Experiment 26

1 Hirshkowitz, M., Whiton, K., Albert, S. M., Alessi, C., Bruni, O., DonCarlos, L., Hazen, N., Herman, J., Katz, E. S., Kheirandish-Gozal, L., Neubauer, D. N., O'Donnell, A. E., Ohayon, M., Peever, J., Rawding, R., Sachdeva, R. C., Setters, B., Vitiello, M. V., Ware, J. C., & Adams Hillard, P. J. (2015). National Sleep Foundation's sleep time duration recommendations: methodology and results summary. *Sleep health, 1*(1), 40–43.

2 Medic, G., Wille, M., & Hemels, M.E. (2017). Short- and long-term health consequences of sleep disruption. *Nature and Science of Sleep, 9*, 151–161.

3 Yuhas, P. (2019). *Blue light isn't the main source of eye fatigue and sleep loss – it's your computer.* [online] Available at: https://theconversation.com/blue-light-isnt-the-main-source-of-eye-fatigue-and-sleep-loss-its-your-computer-124235 [Accessed 1 February 2023].

4 Newsom, R. & Singh, A. (2023). *How blue light affects sleep.* [online] Available at: https://www.sleepfoundation.org/ bedroom-environment/blue-light [Accessed 1 February 2023].

5 Haghayayegh, S., Khoshnevis, S., Smolensky, M., H., Diller, K., R., & Castriotta, R., I. (2019). Before-bedtime passive body heating by warm shower or bath to improve sleep: A systematic review and meta-analysis. *Sleep Medicine Reviews,* 46, 124–135.

Experiment 27

1 Grove-White, E. (2019). *Rapt: Attention and the focused life, by Winifred Gallagher.* [online] Available at: https://www. theglobeandmail.com/arts/books-and-media/rapt-attention-and-the-focused-life-by-winifred-gallagher/article4280295/ [Accessed 24 April 2023].

Experiment 28

1 Trenton, N. (2020). *The Empath Self-Care Blueprint: How to Manage, Navigate, and Thrive in an Overwhelming World.* PKCS Media, Inc.

Experiment 30

1 Cameron, J. (1994). *The Artist's Way.* Souvenir Press Ltd.

Experiment 31

1   Fogg, B. *Find a good spot in your life*. [online] Available at: https://tinyhabits.com/good-spot/ [Accessed 17 March 2023].

What to do next

1   Holden, R. (2011). *What is destination addiction?* [online] Available at: https://www.robertholden.com/blog/what-is-destination-addiction/ [Accessed 7 April 2023].

ACKNOWLEDGEMENTS

Thank you to my editor, Beth Bishop, for answering my millions of questions and holding my hand throughout this process. I'm so thankful to Kirsty who, a long time ago, helped re-ignite my creative spark and encouraged me to just try. Thank you to Karen and Sarah, the best cheerleaders you could wish for. Thanks to my lovely friends (more than I can mention in the word limit!) who have jumped up and down and squealed along with me about this book.

Thank you to my mum, brothers, sister and in-laws (there's a lot of them) who have been so excited for me (and quick to pre order!). And to my nieces and nephews who aren't bothered about what their auntie's up to but might read this one day. I don't have the words, ironically, to fully thank my best friend, soul mate and husband, Col, whose unwavering belief in me sustains me through all the times I struggle to believe in myself. I love you. And thanks to our pup, Bailey, and his insistence on playtime and walkies, regardless of deadlines.

Thank you, dear reader, for choosing to experiment with this book, for being open, brave and willing to try. Future you will thank you for it, promise. And thanks to everyone who's ever read my writing, listened to me speak, taken my courses, attended my workshops, or coached with me – you've walked with me on the journey to this book.

Finally – look, Dad, I wrote a book!

ABOUT THE AUTHOR

Gabrielle Treanor is a certified life and positive psychology coach, writer and podcaster, living with her husband and rescue pup in the Brecon Beacons. She is passionate about helping women feel calmer, more peaceful and happier in their daily life, by tackling the cause of their stress and empowering them to live the life they truly want.

Gabrielle spent 15 years in children's magazine and newspaper publishing, before running her own stationery business for several years. After discovering the world of positive psychology and self-development, and understanding what made a difference to her own overthinking, overdoing overwhelm, Gabrielle began creating and teaching online courses to share her learnings with others. She launched her wellbeing business, gabrielletreanor.com, trained in life and positive psychology coaching and sold her stationery business to focus fully on supporting overwhelmed women to feel more calm and joy.

As well as coaching Gabrielle writes on wellbeing topics for a range of magazines and publications, hosts the Pressing Pause podcast, runs online courses and workshops for individuals and organizations, works with her local mental health charity, and is currently studying a MSc in Applied Positive Psychology.

To find out more about Gabrielle and the support she offers go to gabrielletreanor.com.